CINCINNATI RECIPE TREASURY

Cincinnati

THE QUEEN CITY'S

Recipe

CULINARY HERITAGE

Treasury

MARY ANNA DUSABLON

Ohio University Press

Originally published in 1983 by the Donning Company.

Ohio University Press edition published 1989.

Ohio University Press books are
printed on acid-free paper.

Library of Congress Cataloging in Publication Data

DuSablon, Mary Anna, 1939–
Cincinnati recipe treasury.

Includes index.
1. Cookery, American—Ohio.   2. Cincinnati (Ohio)—
Social life and customs.   I. Title.
TX715.D947   1983   641.59771'78   82-14773
ISBN 0-8214-0933-6

Dedication

To my beloved husband Sean Thomas Bailey who suggested I write a "genuine and generous" book. To my children who still enjoy my Cincinnati cooking—Julia Marcel, the Cincinnati Chili; Jeanmarie, the Poppyseed Cake; Charles Martin, the Goetta; Theresa Rose, the Weenies and Chippie. To my dog Sadie who takes me on walks so I don't get fat.

Contents

Preface

It has been my privilege, a labor of love, to bring together the words and pictures which have made this book a reality. My humble endeavors were made significant by the warm generosity of the people of Cincinnati.

Great cooks abound in Cincinnati—people whose superlative talents flourish virtually unknown outside the circles of family and friends. Occasionally an entrepreneur will gain the courage to open a restaurant or catering service, but more often than not this wealth of culinary art and experience is acknowledged once in a church or club cookbook, or by a resounding cheer at a lodge dinner, and then taken for granted.

There was no human way to contact each of the great cooks recommended to me, nor to reproduce every tasty and traditional recipe. A sincere effort was made nevertheless to represent our town through its cultural heritage, its family traditions, and its creative endeavors, and to reflect the intimacy of real home cooking—a treasury unto itself.

Cincinnatians, an unusually friendly breed, take their food seriously. They are not generally anxious to try new things, but will experiment with encouragement and render an honest opinion. What they like, they like; what they don't like, they never will.

Although they are frugal cooks as a rule, Cincinnatians will make exceptions to create a perfect meal for a special occasion. For this reason many families have dealt with one butcher shop for a lifetime where they have come to expect a superior product. Individuals or church groups will pool their resources to fly lobster in from New England in August or to buy bulk meat at packing plants in order to serve a choice steak to a crowd at a reasonable cost.

This emphasis on quality was inherited from ancestors who built the great Findlay Market building in the heart of the city, which functions today much as it did yesterday. Other elements of a rich culinary heritage were the great vineyards of the past, the lowland farms, and the rising terraces covered with woodland and forest, teeming with wildlife. Cincinnatians learned to cherish good food most at their mothers' and grandmothers' tables, and their contributions to the recorded history of our country is considerable.

For there is much to learn from a cookbook. As in many cities, cookbooks have become a Cincinnati preoccupation; almost every donor of a recipe in this compilation admitted to being a collector. I handled hundreds of these cookbooks while preparing this manuscript, some new and innovative, some old and falling apart, still handed down through generations. Naturally the best cookbooks were the most dog-eared, barely readable under the flour and grease stains of past preparations.

Some of my favorite moments were when little clipped recipes, yellow with age, fell out from between the pages, or when a child's scrawl appeared along with the cook's notations handwritten on the endsheets. Once a perfectly pressed four-leaf-clover was found lying against a recipe for blackberry cake, and I wondered if both clover and berries were found that lucky summer's day.

Each of these books contained a wealth of secret formulas for greater enjoyment of food, and understanding of life as it was when the book was written.

Until the last thirty or so years, most of our local repasts were influenced primarily by our own culture. But lately the world has come to Cincinnati by way of new residents and restaurants, bringing with them menus and recipes that may well be the history of tomorrow.

And so this book becomes part of our present heritage. It contains so few words considering how many lively conversations took place to bring it about. In some cases whole books could be written about a single recipe, or a single donor whose character and personality expanded with her or his ability to "put out a good spread."

A few of these people I must thank for their above-and-beyond assistance during the hundreds of telephone calls soliciting their advice and inspiration. My mother, Bernadette Marcella Martin; Caroline Maxwell, Dutch Maxwell, Therese Hart, Mary Rose Pitzer, Maey Schott, Mary Valerio, and the three girls at Kroger's who courteously answered all my questions of sizes and amounts, Karen Milburn, Annette Lazzele, and Amy Riggo. To my capable and optimistic editor, Robyn Browder, I say thanks, and also to Alex

10

Jackinson, my agent, who procured for me this enviable assignment. Another big thanks to Adam and Marie of Marie's Restaurant. Last, to the memory of my father, Lieutenant Charles Martin (1915-1962), Cincinnati Police Department, who loved and protected this city.

True Cincinnatians will forgive this indulgence, for we are, together or apart, a family-oriented city. And our family room is most often the kitchen.

Beverages

Cincinnati's Union Terminal

Union Terminal. Peak traffic at this elegant structure was reached during World War II when almost 200 trains arrived and departed each day. Drawing by Don Sharpshair, courtesy Row House Gallery, Milford.

Breweries and Wineries

During the mid-1800s there was a rapid growth of German immigrants into Cincinnati. Between 1835 and 1850 the German population grew from 5 percent to 77 percent of the city's total inhabitants. With them came a hearty thirst for lager beer. Among the indoor-outdoor biergartens and stubes there were thirty-six breweries in 1860, and in 1891 Cincinnatians consumed more beer per capita than any other city in the United States.

At the turn of the century, the Wiedemann Brewery claimed in an advertisement that their beer cured "nervousness, fatigue and worry."

However, due to the ravages of competition within the industry, there are only two independently owned breweries in the greater Cincinnati area today, Hudepohl and Schoenling. Still, Cincinnati can boast some of the finest beers in the world, and cold beer is probably the favored drink as it has been since it was toted home from the corner saloon in bailed buckets.

In spite of the hopes of prohibitionists, a great number of Cincinnatians cherish their neighborhood bars as they do their churches, and not irreverently. Friendships have begun over that first legal beer that have endured a lifetime.

Bock beer, that sweet and mysterious dark brew, is enjoyed in early spring. The melodious strains of "Danny Boy" in March give way to "Du, Du Liegst Mir Im Herzen" during Oktoberfest, and all summer there exists the possibility of a free round bought by a patron whose bet was lucky at River Downs Race Track.

Here and there you'll still find a few nostalgists who bring their own beer steins to the tavern to quaff.

Catawba grapes were grown and tended in Cincinnati by those Germans from the Rhineland, where the hill country is not unlike Cincinnati. Much of Eden Park and Mt. Adams was vineyards belonging to Nicholas Longworth. Ohio Valley grapes were used in local winemaking up until the 1950s when The John C. Meier Company vineyards were magically transformed into the Kenwood Shopping Center.

14

The Mt. Adams-Eden Park Incline. A page from Cincinnati's past, the Mt. Adams Incline
was opened for business in 1876. Passengers rode up and down on its two
counterbalanced cars, named "Nicholas Longworth" and "Martin Baum," until 1948.
The city boasted several inclines in the 1800s; this one and the Price Hill-Eighth Street
Incline were the last of this type of transportation to be used. Drawing by Edward
Timothy Hurley, the distinguished Rockwood Pottery artist

Meier's Fiesta Catawba Punch

The famous nonalcoholic "Pink Sparkling Grape Juice" from Meiers Wine Cellars is an unusual beverage, perfect for the entire family. It is naturally sweet and rich in flavor. When it is served alone, everyone can enjoy the excitement of the popping cork and the soft, petal-pink bubbly juice. Served in this old recipe it is pretty and refreshing.

Yield: 40 servings

½ cup lemon juice
1 46-ounce can unsweetened
   pineapple juice, chilled
¾ cup sugar
2 fifths catawba pink sparkling grape

juice, chilled
1 quart sparkling water
Orange slices for garnish
Maraschino cherries or strawberries
   for garnish

Just before serving, place the lemon juice, pineapple juice, and sugar in the punch bowl and stir to dissolve. Add one tray of ice cubes. Stir in the grape juice and sparkling water. Garnish with fruit.

Cincinnati Red

This famous beer recipe from The Hudepohl Brewing Company is suggested as a pickup for breakfast or brunch. Some residents claim it is a good hangover cure.

Yield: 6 servings

12 ounces Hudepohl beer, chilled
12 ounces tomato juice, chilled

Dash cayenne
Dash Worcestershire sauce

Combine the ingredients in a large pitcher. Stir well and serve chilled or over ice.

The Recipe

This is what Cincinnati's Jet Set is drinking at their poolside condominiums in Florida!

Yield: 12 to 15 servings

1 6-ounce can frozen orange juice
1 6-ounce can frozen lemonade
1 46-ounce can pineapple juice
1 2-liter bottle 7-Up

6 bananas or 1 pint strawberries or chopped fresh peaches
½ to 1 pint vodka

Place all the ingredients into a blender and process until thoroughly mixed. Freeze and serve like a slush, keeping the unused portion in the freezer.

—Helen Miller
Grosbeck

Hop Beer

Put to five quarts of water six ounces of hops, boil three hours; then strain off the liquor and put to the hops four more quarts of water, four or five raw potatoes pared and sliced, a half pint ginger, and boil the hops two hours longer. Then strain and mix it with the rest of the liquor, stirring in a couple quarts of molasses. Take half a pound of rusked bread, pound it fine, and brown it in a pot over the fire, stirring it constantly. Slices of bread toasted very brown will do, but are not as good as the rusked bread to enrich the beer. Add it to the liquor, and when cool, so as to be just lukewarm, stir in a pint of fresh made yeast, that has no salt in it, as the salt keeps it from fermenting readily. Keep the beer covered in a temperate situation till the fermentation ceases, which is ascertained by the subsiding of the froth. Then turn it off carefully into a beer-keg, jugs, or bottles. The bottles should not be corked tight, as the beer will be apt to burst them. Keep the beer in a cool place.

—The American Kitchen Directory and
Housewife, *by Anne Howe,* 1868

Compound Wine

An excellent family wine may be made of equal parts of red, white and black currants, ripe cherries and raspberries well bruised and mixed with soft water, in the proportion of four pounds of fruit to one gallon of water. When strained and pressed, three pounds of moist sugar are to be added to each gallon of the liquid. After straining, open for three days, during which it is to be stirred frequently; it is to be put in a barrel, and left for two weeks to work, when a ninth part of brandy is to be added, and the whole bunged down. In a few months it will be a most excellent wine, inferior to none.

—The House-Keeper's Guide and Everybody's Handbook
*by Smith and Swinney, Chemists; stereotyped
at the Franklin Type Foundry, Cincinnati,* 1864

Hot Spiced Cider

Rouster's Apple House, east of Milford, is familiar to most Cincinnatians. The Rouster Family bought a small orchard, planted more trees, and established an apple truck delivery route through the eastern hills during the depression. The family's old log house now serves as a "country store" for homemade jellies, jams, butters, conserves, sauces, eggs, fruits, berries, and their trademark, the "Krispy" apple. Developed and sold only at Rouster's, the Krispy is unique in that it is equally excellent as a cooking, baking, preserving, and eating apple.

Yield: 1 gallon

1 gallon Rouster's apple cider	2 cinnamon sticks
4 tablespoons honey	½ lemon, unpeeled
12 whole cloves	Cinnamon sticks (optional)

Place all of the ingredients in a large pot, stir well, and simmer for ten minutes. Strain. Serve in mugs, with a cinnamon stick if desired.

18

Silverton Special

This is another unique drink from Meier's Wine Cellars in Silverton, Ohio, combining their still nonalcoholic grape juice with spirits.

Yield: 1 serving

1 jigger whiskey
Dash grenadine
Meier's catawba grape juice

Sparkling water
Lemon slice for garnish

Place three ice cubes in a small glass. Add the whiskey and grenadine. Then fill the glass with equal amounts of grape juice and sparkling water. Stir briskly and garnish with a lemon slice.

French Minted Iced Tea

Yield: about 9 cups concentrate

13 tea bags
1/4 cup chopped mint leaves
2 quarts water, divided
Juice of 2 lemons

1 6-ounce can orange juice
   concentrate, thawed
1 cup sugar
Mint sprigs for garnish

Combine tea bags, mint leaves, and 1 quart of water. Bring to a boil. Remove from the heat and steep 30 minutes. Add juices, sugar, and 1 quart of additional water. Strain and serve over lots of crystal-clear ice with a mint sprig garnish.

—Lauretta Omeltschenko

Hall Deckers' Reward

For many years this has been served at the Frame home on Christmas Eve, tree-trimming time.

Yield: 6 servings

3 1-ounce squares unsweetened
   chocolate
1/2 cup sugar
1/2 cup cold water

1/2 teaspoon salt
1/2 cup heavy cream
1 to 2 teaspoons vanilla extract
1 quart hot milk

Combine chocolate, sugar, water, and salt in a small saucepan. Heat and stir on a low heat, until the chocolate is melted and the mixture is thick and smooth. Remove from heat and cool completely. Whip the cream until stiff and blend in the vanilla. Gently fold the chocolate mixture into the whipped cream and pile lightly into an attractive serving bowl. Store in the refrigerator until ready to use. To serve, heat the milk just to scalding (do not boil). Pour hot milk into a heat-proof pitcher. Into your prettiest cups, put a heaping tablespoon of the chocolate-cream mixture and fill the cup with hot milk.

—Marjorie A. Frame
Anderson Township Historical Society

Hot Ginger Ale

Vernor's Ginger Ale, now bottled by Barq's, has been in Cincinnati since 1866. This recipe was attached to the bottles in 1954. Any ginger ale can probably be used for this recipe, but it might not have the same old hometown flavor.

Here's a treat as original and surprising as the famous Vernor's flavor itself. Heat Vernor's to the boiling point in a glass or metal container, then pour over a small piece of lemon. It's especially welcome on a cold day after outdoor activity.

Dandelion Wine

Yield: about 1 gallon

1 gallon dandelion blossoms, packed but not bruised	3 oranges
1 lemon	4 pounds sugar
	1 package wine yeast

Pick the dandelions when they are wide open early on a bright, sunny morning. Remove stems and leaves, discarding as much of the green as possible. Pour 1 gallon of boiling water over the blossoms. Allow to stand for 3 days then add the juice and rinds of the lemon and oranges. Stir in the sugar and the yeast. At the end of 10 days, use plastic tubing to strain into a carboy under a water seal, being sure not to leave any sugar in the vat. When the wine comes clear it may be bottled, usually in 2 to 3 weeks. This is a sweet wine with a great floral smell.

Note: Carboys, water seals, and tubing can be purchased at a wine supply store.

—Stephene Raider
Oxford

Water

Water, vital to any culture and particularly stressed in European cultures, may have gained some of its singular local popularity through a book originally published in Woerishofen, Bavaria around 1886. It was titled *The Kneipp Cure*, or *My Water Cure*, in America. There were at least sixty-two German editions, and a few copies, both in German and English, found their way into Cincinnati homes.

The author was a priest whose "patients" included Pope Leo XIII, Empress Fredericka of Germany, Empress Elizabeth of Austria, the Prince of Wales who later became King Edward VIII, and the Baron Rothschild.

Along with directions on how to drink water were suggestions for baths, vapor baths, shower baths, etc.

His creed was:

Drink as often as you are thirsty, and never drink much!

If you are thirsty before meals, well, then drink! The thirst announces a want of juices.

At a table do not drink at all, or very little, in order that the purest gastric juice may soak and penetrate all, even the last mouthful of food.

If, a good time after meals, the food mixture again wants some fluid to help the stomach to digestion. . .you may drink, but moderately.

The drink should be the genuine beverage offered by God in every well. (I am not a Puritan and allow gladly a glass of wine or beer, but without regarding them as important as they are commonly believed to be.)

Nectar Soda

Pharmacists on both sides of the river claimed to originate this heavenly flavor, in the 1940s. Ice-cream shops still feature this item but no longer serve it with a silver spoon.

1 pint cold milk
1 cup sugar
1 ounce (2 tablespoons) vanilla extract
1 dram (about 1 teaspoon) lemon extract
1 dram (about 1 teaspoon) orange extract
few drops red coloring
carbonated water
vanilla ice-cream

Combine the milk and sugar, then agitate (druggist's word for stir) to dissolve. Add flavors and agitate again. Add red coloring. (You'll have to experiment, a Nectar Soda should be a delicate rose blush pink.) Into a 12-ounce glass put two ounces of the syrup. Add a fine stream of carbonated water to half fill the glass and cause the syrup to foam. Add two scoops of vanilla ice-cream. Add enough carbonated water to fill the glass, agitating with a long-shank spoon to give it a fine fluff on top. (Syrup will keep about three days in the refrigerator.)

—E. L. Pieck
Pieck's Pharmacy, Covington

Snacks and Appetizers

TYLER DAVIDSON FOUNTAIN - 1970
CINCINNATI

Tyler Davidson Fountain, 1970. The fountain was presented to the people of Cincinnati in 1871 by Henry Probasco as a memorial to his brother-in-law Tyler Davidson. It was cast by Ferdinand von Muller of the Royal Bronze Foundry of Bavaria following plans drawn by August von Kreling. The nine-foot central figure, the Genius of Water, stands with arms outstretched over groupings of figures "in which all the manifold uses and blessings of water were symbolized and embodied." The fountain is located in Fountain Square, where downtown workers brown-bag their lunches while enjoying noon hour concerts during summer months. Drawing by Steve Mueller

23

Pretzels

In years gone by these warm, doughy mouthfuls were sold in brown bags from steaming wagons at Fountain Square, Findlay Market, 8th and State, Knowlton's Corner, and other sites. Perhaps because the pretzels were "big," they were called "bretzels" by many folk.

Yield: 30 to 35 long pretzels or 25 twist pretzels

1 cake or package of yeast	2 tablespoons lye
1¼ cups warm water	Coarse salt to taste
4½ cups unsifted white flour	

Dissolve the yeast in the warm water. Pour this over the flour and mix until all of the flour is gone. (Do not add more water.) Cover and set aside to rise in a warm place for half an hour. Then knead and shape into long or twist pretzels. Put the lye into two quarts of cold water in an enamel pan and bring to a boil. Grease a baking sheet. Keeping the water just at the boiling point, dip the pretzels in the water and then place them on the baking sheet. Sprinkle with the coarse salt. Bake at 375 degrees F. for 10 to 12 minutes. Serve hot, with mustard if desired.

Note: The use of lye in this recipe gives the pretzel a shiny coating which cannot be duplicated in any other way. Some frown upon this practice, but most pretzel lovers laugh and proclaim "at least you know what's in it!"

—Audrey Reinhart
Mt. Washington

Onion Butter Bites

At many home demonstrations Ann Holiday would quickly prepare these tasty morsels. Every homemaker who tasted them immediately requested the recipe.

Yield: 40

½ package onion soup mix	10 buttermilk biscuits, unbaked
½ cup (1 stick) butter or margarine	

Stir the onion soup powder before dividing it to distribute all the seasonings. Melt the butter, then mix in the soup to make a sauce. Cut each biscuit into four pieces with kitchen shears. Place the biscuit bits in a greased 5-by-9-inch baking dish. Cover with the sauce. Bake at 450 degrees F. for 10 to 12 minutes or until golden.

—Ann Holiday
The Cincinnati Gas and Electric Company/
The Union Light, Heat and Power Company

Sauerkraut Balls

Cincinnatians eat cabbage and kraut in any fashion; this is a recent innovation.

Yield: 30–35 walnut-sized balls

1 pound sauerkraut
1/4 pound ham, cooked
1/4 pound corned beef, cooked
1/2 pound pork sausage, uncooked
1/3 cup minced onions

1/2 cup white flour
1/2 teaspoon salt
1/2 teaspoon dry mustard
White flour, for coating

Batter

1 egg beaten
2/3 milk

3/4 teaspoon salt
Dry breadcrumbs, for coating

Drain and squeeze the sauerkraut, saving the juice, and chop finely. Grind the ham and corned beef through the fine plate of a food grinder, or in a food processor, and set aside. In a heavy skillet, fry the sausage and onions until lightly browned, breaking the meat into small pieces. Add the ground ham and corned beef to the sausage and onion mixture and cook until heated through. Sift the flour, salt, and mustard together and add all at once to the meat mixture, stirring constantly to combine. Add 2/3 cup of sauerkraut juice, stirring constantly, and cook 3 to 5 minutes or until thickened. Remove from heat. Add the drained and chopped sauerkraut and mix well. Chill overnight in the refrigerator.

Shape into walnut-size balls. To make the batter, mix the egg, milk, and salt. Dip each ball in flour to coat well, then dip it in the batter, and roll it in the breadcrumbs. The sauerkraut balls may be frozen now for later use or deep fried at 360 degrees F. and served with toothpicks. Break one when slightly browned to be sure the center is heated. If it is too brown outside and raw inside, reduce the heat.

—Joy Pitzer
Western Hills

Antipasto

From Valerio's family restaurant, a colorful part of Cincinnati's history from 1919 until 1961, this recipe was designed to delight the eye and whet the appetite.

Yield: 2 servings

Marinated Artichokes

1 8-ounce can whole hearts of artichokes
1 teaspoon lemon juice
Several strips lemon peel
2 tablespoons olive oil
5 paper-thin slices onion or shallots

1 garlic clove, pierced on a toothpick
Salt and freshly ground pepper to taste
Pinch sugar
Pinch oregano

Antipasto

3 tablespoons sliced pimento
3 cups shredded lettuce, endive, or watercress
Italian dressing
1 7-ounce can tuna, drained
1 tablespoon olive oil

½ small onion or shallot
Black olives for garnish
8 to 10 paper-thin slices Italian salami
2 slices provolone cheese

Drain artichokes and reserve juice. If the artichokes are large, carefully cut in half. Place in a bowl, add all of the remaining marinade ingredients, and toss together gently, using folding strokes to prevent bruising or breaking the delicate artichoke leaves. Cover and refrigerate for several days, but remove the garlic after one day. At intervals, swirl the contents (with the lid on) to marinate thoroughly.

Note: These marinated artichokes may be eaten on hors d'oeuvre picks, as an antipasto, or placed on a bed of lettuce.

Marinate the pimento overnight in a little olive oil to which a little salt, sliced garlic, and finely chopped parsley have been added. To assemble the antipasto, place the lettuce on a flat serving dish and dribble lightly with Italian dressing. Place the tuna in the center, and spread a tablespoon of olive oil over it. Cut the onion or shallot into paper-thin slices, divide into rings, and place over the tuna. Circle the pimento slices around the tuna, then circle the artichokes around the pimento. Edge with scattered black olives, surround by salami slices folded in half and the provolone cheese cut in pie-shaped pieces.

—Mary Valerio
Hyde Park

Saganaki

A dramatic Greek appetizer, this one is brought to the table flaming!

Yield: 2 servings

1 egg
2 tablespoons milk
1½ to 1-inch slice Kefaloteri, Kaseri, Haloumi, or Parmesan cheese

Flour for coating
2 tablespoons olive oil
1 ounce brandy
½ lemon

Beat the egg and milk together in a bowl. Dip the cheese slice into the mixture, then into the flour. Heat the oil in a small skillet until tiny bubbles begin to rise. Fry the cheese until browned, 3 to 5 minutes on each side. Pour brandy over the cheese and light. Carry the skillet to the table while it is flaming and with a flourish shout "Opa!" (Hurrah) and put out the flame with a squeeze of lemon juice. This fried cheese is exquisite served alone or with toast or crackers.

—George Kalomeres
Kennedy Heights

Liptauer Spread

This Austrian-Viennese family appetizer was given to us by the editor of one of Cincinnati's best collections of recipes, the *Angel's Food Cookbook,* published by Guardian Angel Church in 1974.

Yield: 8 to 10 servings

1 8-ounce package cream cheese
6 tablespoons butter or margarine
½ cup sour cream
1 teaspoon paprika
2 teaspoons caraway seed
1 teaspoon dry mustard
1 tablespoon minced onion
¼ teaspoon salt

⅛ teaspoon pepper
3 tablespoons chopped chives
1 loaf dark rye bread
1 3-ounce bottle capers, drained
12 to 15 radishes, sliced
1 bunch green onions, cut into 1-inch lengths

Allow the cream cheese and butter to soften. Then place the sour cream in the blender, adding the cream cheese, butter, paprika, caraway, mustard, onion, salt, and pepper; blend until smooth. Pack into a bowl or shape into a ball and decorate with the chives. Refrigerate for at least two hours. Serve with mounds of torn rye bread, capers, radishes, and onions.

—Betty Wester

Taramosalata

This Greek savory pink appetizer begins with tarama, red caviar. It is not an expensive roe, and the ingredients can be combined to your personal taste. The traditional version used fresh breadcrumbs or mashed potatoes, depending on the area in Greece the cook is from, combined with olive oil. However, a mildly flavored alternative is the substitution of cream cheese whipped in the blender for some of the oil.

Yield: approximately 2½ cups

1 4-ounce jar tarama
¼ cup water
1 cup fresh breadcrumbs or mashed potatoes

Juice of 1 lemon or lime
½ onion, chopped
1 cup olive oil or cream cheese

Place the tarama, water, breadcrumbs, lemon juice, and onion in the blender in the order given and process until well combined. Add the olive oil slowly and blend into a smooth paste. Taste for seasonings. Chill and use as a dip or spread.

—George Kalomeres
Kennedy Heights

Rye Bread-Beer Cheese Dip

"I got this recipe from a girlfriend who got it from another girlfriend. It's always the first hors d'oeuvre to disappear at parties," says Rita.

Yield: 1 loaf

1 cup beer
1 pound sharp Cheddar cheese, chopped
2 ounces bleu cheese, crumbled
2 tablespoons butter or margarine
½ medium onion, chopped fine

2 garlic cloves, chopped fine
1 teaspoon Worcesterhire sauce
¼ teaspoon hot sauce
1 loaf round Swedish rye bread
1 loaf dark rye bread

Heat the beer just to the boiling point and set aside to cool. Mix cheeses with margarine, onion, and garlic. Add Worcestershire sauce and hot sauce. Add a small amount of the cooled beer and beat with an electric mixer at low speed. Slowly add the remaining beer, gradually increasing the speed of the mixer until the mixture is the consistency of mayonnaise. Spoon into a glass jar and cover. It will keep refrigerated for several days. To serve cut out a fist-sized hole in the top of the round loaf. Hollow out the interior, leaving a ''crust'' of about one inch on the bottom and sides. Cut this leftover bread, as well as the loaf of dark rye, into one-inch cubes. Pour the cold mixture into the hollowed-out loaf, or warm the mixture first, stirring constantly, without boiling. Place the bread cubes around the loaf-dip to dunk. Serve immediately.

—Rita Ennis
Anderson Township

Oysters in Sherry Cream

Oyster dishes have always been popular with religious families during meat-fasting holidays. An old Meier's Wine Cellar promotional claims that this dish will ''send supper or luncheon appetites soaring.''

Yield: 4 servings

1 cup heavy cream	temperature
¼ cup sherry wine	Salt and pepper to taste
1 quart oysters, drained and at room	½ cup breadcrumbs, buttered

Warm a shallow baking dish in a 350 degree F. oven for five minutes. Place the cream in a small pan and heat to the boiling point. Add the sherry. Pour this mixture into the baking dish. Add the drained oysters, spreading them out evenly. Sprinkle with salt and pepper. Over the top scatter the breadcrumbs. Broil for about five minutes or until the edges of the oysters curl up and the crumbs are browned slightly.

Pimento Cheese Spread

Always found in the delicatessens, this is easy and delicious to make.

12 ounces Cheddar or American cheese	Dash hot sauce
	Dash salt
1 4-ounce jar pimento, chopped	Mayonnaise as needed
1 teaspoon Worcestershire sauce	

29

Set the cheese out until it is at room temperature, then chop it finely. In a bowl place the cheese, pimento, and seasonings. Toss lightly, then add enough mayonnaise to make a good spreading consistency. Store covered in the refrigerator. Serve with crackers.

—Mabel Wallace
Mt. Washington

Steak Tartar

This recipe was created for The Plaza in Paris, France, by Chef Gregory, former owner of the Celestial Restaurant in Mt. Adams, and Hyde Park cooking instructor. This popular and talented chef now works and resides in Columbus, Indiana.

Yield: 8 servings

2 pounds very lean, freshly ground
    filet, sirloin round steak, no fat
1 medium onion, chopped
Four friends*
1 tablespoon Dijon mustard
2 tablespoons olive oil
Salt to taste

Ground black pepper to taste
2 ounces oil-packed anchovies
2 to 3 eggs
¼ cup brandy or cognac
¼ cup capers, drained
½ cup finely chopped fresh parsley

Place the beef into a bowl. Into the blender jar place the onion, four friends, mustard, olive oil, salt, pepper, anchovies, eggs, and liquor. Blend on medium speed until all is combined and then add to the beef. Add the capers and parsley and carefully blend all of the ingredients together as if you are making a meat loaf. *Do not overwork.* This may be put into an oiled glass or ceramic mold, covered securely and refrigerated, or served immediately. Serve with sour rye or dark rye bread.

*Four friends are: 1 teaspoon *each* of garlic salt, Accent or MSG, and liquid Maggi, plus one drop Tabasco.

—James Gregory
The Chef Gregory Cookbook, 1972

30

Wurstsalat

This old recipe turns out only as good as the quality of bologna used to make it. It is shared by Charlene, daughter of "Best Cook" Elsie Firstos (see Sauerbraten). Charlene is an excellent cook and hostess herself, and editor of two superb Our Lady of Visitation cookbooks.

Yield: 6 to 8 servings

1 pound German bologna or leona
1 onion, chopped fine
1 dill pickle, chopped fine
⅓ cup vinegar

⅓ cup salad oil
1 teaspoon salt
1 teaspoon mustard
1 tablespoon minced fresh parsley

Cut the sausage into very small pieces or julienne strips and place in a bowl. Combine the remaining ingredients and pour over the sausage. Mix gently. Refrigerate overnight or at least 12 hours. Serve with crackers or party rye bread.

—Charlene Dittrich
Western Hills

Bay Scallop-Smoked Salmon Mousse with Beurre Blanc

Yield: 5 servings

Salmon Mousse

11 ounces bay scallops, drained
5 ounces smoked salmon
2 egg whites
1 teaspoon salt (varies with saltiness

of smoked salmon)
½ teaspoon white pepper
2 cups heavy cream

Beurre Blanc

⅓ cup white wine vinegar
⅓ cup dry white wine
2 shallots, chopped fine

Salt and white pepper
1 cup soft, unsalted butter

Preheat the oven to 400 degrees F. In a food processor purée the bay scallops, smoked salmon, egg whites, salt, and white pepper for 30 seconds. With the food processor still running, add the cream in a stream over a time span of about 30 seconds. Grease five 1-cup mousse molds. Fill

31

molds up to ¼-inch from the top. Bake in a pan filled with one inch of water for 25 minutes or until lightly brown on top. Meanwhile, prepare the Beurre Blanc. Simmer all of the ingredients except the butter until only 3 tablespoons of liquid are left. Over very low heat, add 2 tablespoons of the butter at a fast whisk. A light buttery emulsion should occur after all the butter has been added. When the mousse are done, remove from the oven and from the water pan, and cool 5 to 10 minutes. Invert on individual appetizer plates and serve with the Beurre Blanc, plus an additional fresh tomato sauce if desired.

—Chef Dan Eyink
Mecklenburg Gardens

Chipped Beef-Cream Cheese Ball

Cheese balls became very popular during the 1950s. Every family has its own recipe on file and this favorite one comes from the Machenheimer Family.

Yield: 1 cheese ball

1 6-ounce package chipped beef	1 teaspoon Worcestershire sauce
1 8-ounce package cream cheese	1 teaspoon horseradish
5 tablespoons chopped green onion	Salt and pepper to taste

Divide the package of chipped beef in half, reserving one half and chopping the other finely. Place the chopped beef in a small bowl and add the other ingredients. Blend until smooth. Form into a ball and flatten slightly. Use the remaining chipped beef to coat the cheese ball. Serve with crackers.

Note: For a festive look, chop up all the chipped beef and blend it into the cheese mixture. Cover the cheese ball with paprika and parsley flakes.

—Sue Machenheimer
Anderson Township

Cracklin's
(Pork Rinds)

This very old German recipe comes from the owner of Findlay Market Stall #10. He is a sausage maker, arrived from Germany in 1960; not many people make cracklin's these days, but this is the traditional, and best, recipe.

The best cracklin's are made from the fat attached to the pork loin, although many people use any of the pork fat with the skin taken off. How much you get depends on how fat the pig is, but there is usually 1½ to 3 pounds of this choice fat. Using a filet knife, cut the fat away from the loin. Then cut the fat into big chunks. Render them down slowly on a low heat, being careful not to burn. (Cook as you would bacon.) Pour off the liquid as it accumulates; this is a fine lard and can be refrigerated and used as shortening in any recipe. When the fat is completely rendered, what is left are the cracklin's. From approximately 10 pounds of fat you might get two pounds of cracklin's. Salt them for a crisp snack, or break them up to be added to cornbread batter.

—Paul Kroeger
Findlay Market

Party Cold Cuts

Many Kahn cookbooks were distributed throughout Cincinnati by the century-old company. These items, from a chapter titled "Kahn's American Beauty Table Ready Meats," appeared in a booklet which was probably printed in the early 50s. It included an introduction by local food expert Fran Storer.

New England Luncheon Loaf Sandwich Spread

Grind ¼ pound Kahn's American Beauty New England Luncheon Loaf and combine with three chopped hard-cooked eggs, and three chopped sweet pickles. Combine with mayonnaise.

Pickle Loaf and Pepper Loaf Cornucopias

Roll slices of Kahn's Pickle Loaf or Pepper Loaf into cone shapes, fasten with toothpicks, and fill with well-seasoned cottage cheese, cabbage slaw, baked beans, or potato salad.

Liver Sausageburgers

Cut Kahn's Long Liver Sausage in ½-inch slices and brown slightly in small amount of fat. Serve with onion rings and tomato slices on hot toasted buns.

Thuringer Sausage and Salami Salad

Cut Kahn's Thuringer Sausage or Salami or both into long, slender strips and add to crisp vegetable salads just before serving. OR: cut in small cubes and add to kidney bean, potato, or macaroni salad.

Kahn's Meat Cookery
The E. Kahn's Sons Co.

Salads and Salad Dressings

Cincinnati Riverfront Stadium—home of the 1982 & 1989 National Football League Superbowl contenders, the Cincinnati Bengals. Home also to the Cincinnati Reds who have won four National League pennants and two World Series since the facility opened in July, 1970. Seating capacity for loyal fans is 54,700 for baseball games, and 59,750 for football games. The entire site encompasses forty-eight acres, including 123,000 square feet of astroturf. Drawing by Caroline Williams

Cincinnati Picnic Menu

This menu is a typical family picnic smorgasboard, with family members bringing the dishes for which they are famous. These picnics are held in Alms or Ault Park, Winton Woods, Whitewater Forest, or more than likely in the biggest backyard the family boasts. Many such feasts have been held in the Wallace family backyard on the Fourth of July from the 1930s to the present. Besides playing yard games of all types, the group usually listened to the Reds play ball. Mabel Wallace, in her seventies, and a lifelong Cincinnati Reds fan, watches the games now from a VIP seat. Granddaughter Jackie married shortstop Ron Oester in 1980.

Fried Chicken

Brats n' Metts   . . .for the grill. . .   Weiners

Yellow Mustard   Fresh Horseradish   German Mustard

Bakery Buns

Sliced Garden Tomatoes   Thinly Sliced Cucumbers

Green Onions

Cherry Belle Radishes   Hot Icicle Radishes

German Hot Potato Salad

Mom's Potato Salad

Baked Beans

Vinegar Cole Slaw   Creamy Cole Slaw

Dill Pickles, Green Olives, Stuffed Olives, Black Olives,
Sour Pickles, Sweet Pickles, Sweet Onions, Mild Peppers,
Pickled Assorted Vegetables, Mustard Pickles

Deviled Eggs   Macaroni Salad

Pickled Beets, Onions, Hard-Cooked Eggs

Potato Chips   Pretzels

Beer on Tap
Pop iced in the galvanized tubs
Aunt Mary's Blackberry Cake
Aunt Caroline's Coca-Cola Cake

36

"Where are the pickled eggs? How the heck can we have a family reunion without pickled eggs? Who was supposed to bring them?

—*Bob Alfieri*
1983 Maxwell Family Picnic

Pickled Beets and Eggs

This one gets the vote for Cincinnati's most widely-known unusual recipe. After the mixture sits overnight, the eggs are bright purple. Sliced in a salad or used as deviled eggs they are lovely. Some eat the eggs with a drop or two of Worcestershire sauce on the yolk. This offers a wise solution after Easter when there are multitudes of hard-cooked eggs sitting around waiting for a recipe.

Yield: 8 to 10 servings

6 to 8 hard-cooked eggs
2 16-ounce cans small whole beets,
    slices, or wedges
1 cup cider vinegar
1 to 1½ cups sugar

2 cinnamon sticks
2 whole cloves
2 black peppercorns
¼ teaspoon salt
1 large onion, sliced thickly

Carefully crackle the shells for peeling, without gouging the eggs. Peel beneath cool running water to help ease off the shells. Drain the juice from the beets into a measuring cup and add enough water to equal two cups of liquid. Pour the liquid into a saucepan and add the vinegar, sugar, cinnamon, cloves, peppercorns, and salt. Bring to a boil, and then set aside. Place the beets, eggs, and onion slices into a large-mouth jar or a non-metallic bowl, alternating ingredients. Pour the liquid over, cover, and refrigerate overnight. To serve as a relish or salad, drain off the pickling liquid or remove as many eggs and vegetables from the jar or bowl as needed. Slice the eggs in half and surround with the tangy, chilled beets and onion rings.

Note: To use fresh beets (about 1½ pounds) reserve two cups of the cooking liquid and add no water. Although the mixture will keep for several weeks, the eggs and onions tend to get rubbery after a few days.

—Joyce Rosencrans
Food Editor, *The Cincinnati Post*

Fresh Green Bean Salad

This recipe has been passed through three generations in the LaRosa family. It is still used in the Italian Inn in Western Hills.

Yield: 6 servings

1½ pounds green beans
½ cup wine vinegar
6 ounces roasted red pepper, cut in
  julienne strips
1½ cups olive oil

1 large garlic clove, chopped
2 teaspoons basil
1 teaspoon oregano
1 teaspoon salt
1 teaspoon sugar

Clean and boil the green beans in plenty of water until fork tender, 10 to 15 minutes. Remove and shock in ice water for five minutes. Drain well, place in a bowl and add all of the other ingredients. Toss well, cover, and let marinate overnight. Serve chilled.

—Mark LaRosa
Italian Inn Manager

Hot Dutch Macaroni Salad

In Cincinnati the word "Dutch" is a derivative of *Deutsch*, meaning German. A person nicknamed Dutch is said to be stubborn or headstrong.

Yield: 6 servings

2 cups elbow macaroni
8 slices bacon
¼ cup sugar
1½ teaspoons dry mustard
1½ teaspoons celery seed
1 teaspoon salt

½ cup vinegar
2 eggs, beaten
½ cup chopped onions
½ cup chopped celery
1 red and green mango
  (green pepper), cut in thin strips

Boil the macaroni in salted water according to package directions. Drain. In a medium size skillet, fry the bacon until crisp. Remove, cool, and crumble. Pour off all but about ¼ cup of the drippings. Add the sugar, dry mustard, celery seed, and salt to the warm fat and stir well. Add the vinegar, mix well, and then bring to a boil. Place the eggs in a small bowl and add a little of the hot vinegar to prevent curdling. Then add the eggs to the vinegar mixture. Cook until smooth and thick, stirring constantly. Combine the macaroni, bacon pieces, onions, celery, and mango. Pour the vinegar mixture over the salad and mix well. Serve warm or at room temperature.

Note: This dressing can be used to make Hot German Potato Salad.

—Mary Rose Pitzer

Sweetbread Salad

Sweetbreads, that part of the animal at the base of the throat, were extremely popular in years gone by, particularly those from calves. Butchers rarely "see them to sell them" nowadays as they are removed to sell to restaurants. The going price in Cincinnati is about six dollars a pound. Sweetbreads were, and still are, considered a delicacy.

Yield: 6 servings

1 pair of sweetbreads	½ cup chopped celery
1 cup French dressing	1 pound fresh peas, boiled
1 tablepoon finely chopped onion	Mayonnaise to taste

Boil the sweetbreads. Cool, skin, and chop them. In a bowl place the French dressing, onion, celery, and peas. Mix carefully, then add the sweetbreads. Chill at least three hours in the ice-box. Mix in a little mayonnaise before serving. Serve with cold asparagus or sliced tomatoes.

—Eva L. Cleveland
Glendale Cookbook, 1935

Layered Salad

Layered, lightly marinated salads are a beautiful and popular innovation, often served in clear glass bowls. The most familiar recipe contains lettuce, ham, spinach, peas, and Swiss cheese. This variation appeared in Our Lady of Visitation Church's excellent cookbook, published in honor of the Bicentennial.

Yield: 6 servings

1 head lettuce	¼ cup sugar
1 large Bermuda onion	2 cups mayonnaise
1 pound bacon	⅓ cup grated Parmesan cheese
1 head cauliflower	Salt and pepper to taste

Cut up the lettuce and thinly slice the onion. Fry the bacon and break it into pieces. Cut the cauliflower into flowerettes. Mix together the sugar, mayonnaise, Parmesan, salt, and pepper. Layer lettuce, bacon, onion, and cauliflower in a bowl one day before serving. Put the mayonnaise dressing over the top. Cover tightly. Stir before serving.

—Marge Walters
The Dinner Bell, 1976

Wilted Dandelion Salad

A beloved early spring ritual, this salad is chock-full of vitamins and minerals. Gather the bright young leaves before flowering or they will turn bitter. All of the leaf is edible and the buds, those tiny rosettes nestled at the base of the plant, are delicious in the salad or boiled and served with oil and vinegar. The best dandelions are found along hillsides poking up from underneath a leafy mulch. Take along a grocery bag and a sharp knife. When you find the dandelion, slip the knife underneath the plant and cut it free from its root. Hold it at the bottom, shake off all excess dirt and leaves, and place it in the bag.

Yield: 1 to 4 servings, depending on how long it has been
since you had dandelions last.

1 to 1½ pounds dandelions
6 green onions or 1 small onion
6 strips bacon
3 tablespoons sugar or honey
½ teaspoon dry mustard
¼ to ½ cup vinegar

½ teaspoon salt
2 hard-cooked eggs, chopped
  (optional)
2 small boiled potatoes, chopped
  (optional)

Fill a large basin or bucket full of water. Place the dandelions in, swish them around a few seconds, and let them sit a minute or two. Remove and drain. Repeat with new water. Then remove the dandelions one by one, separating and cleaning them if necessary. As often as possible, the dandelions should be left intact. Pull off any dead or discolored leaves. Drain in a colander or place in a pillowslip and twirl outside to remove all of the excess water. Set aside. Chop the onion and toss it in with the dandelions. Fry the bacon in a skillet until crisp. Remove and crumble the bacon, and then set aside. Place the sugar or honey and the mustard into the bacon grease and stir until smooth. Add the vinegar and salt and mix well. While still hot, pour over the dandelions and mix thoroughly. Add the bacon, eggs, and potatoes, tossing well. Serve immediately or let stand on the stove until serving time.

Note: This recipe can also be followed for endive, leaf lettuce, shredded cabbage, spinach, or mixed greens.

—Therese Hart (Aunt Dee-dee)
Mt. Washington

Mom's Potato Salad

Every old-fashioned picnic in Cincinnati has at least two potato salads and two cole slaws, the "German-Hot-Vinegar" and the "American-Creamy-Mayonnaise." This is a popular version of the American.

Yield: 8 to 12 servings

8 large red potatoes
8 eggs
1 onion, chopped
2 stalks celery and leaves, chopped fine
1 tablespoon chopped parsley
1 cup chopped cucumbers (optional)

1½ to 2 cups mayonnaise, sour cream, or a combination
1 tablespoon mustard (optional)
Salt and pepper to taste
Leaf lettuce
Paprika and parsley for garnish

Boil the potatoes and eggs in the same pot until the potatoes are just done. When cooled, peel the potatoes and chop them. Peel and chop all but two of the eggs. Place the chopped potatoes and eggs in a large bowl and add the onion, celery, and parsley. Add the cucumbers if desired. Pile the mayonnaise or whatever you choose on top, add the mustard, and toss until everything is well coated. Add more dressing if needed, and then salt and pepper to taste. Line an attractive serving bowl with lettuce leaves and then pile in the potato salad, using a spatula. The curly ends of the lettuce leaves should protrude about an inch above the salad. Top with slices of the remaining hard-cooked eggs, placing them in a circular pattern, or an oval pattern if the bowl is oval. Sprinkle a little parsley on top and sprinkle paprika over the eggs.

Note: Instead of cucumbers, some people add a finely chopped dill pickle or a handful of chopped dandelion greens.

—Bernadette Martin
Mt. Washington

Many families have owed their prosperity full as much to the propriety of female management, as to the knowledge and activity of the father.
—Mrs. J. S. Bradley's Housekeeper's Guide, 1853

Tomato Cheese Gelatin Mold

Yield: 6 servings

1 12-ounce can tomato soup
1 3-ounce package cream cheese
1 envelope unflavored gelatin
1 cup chopped celery

½ cup chopped onion
¼ cup chopped cucumber
¼ pound chopped nuts
1 cup mayonnaise

Blend the soup and cheese together and bring to a boil. Add the gelatin which has been dissolved in one cup of cold water, then set aside to cool. Add all of the other ingredients, folding in the mayonnaise last. Place in a large oiled ring mold and serve with mayonnaise when cold.

—Mrs. John Tarbill
Glendale Cookbook, 1935

Red Cabbage

Yield: 6 to 8 servings

1 large head red cabbage
3 tablespoons butter
1 tablespoon vinegar

1 tablespoon sugar
Red currant jelly
Salt and pepper

Shred the cabbage small. Melt the butter in a pan large enough to hold the cabbage, place it in the pan. Sprinkle it with the vinegar and sugar. Simmer it without burning for about one hour, adding some jelly after it has begun to cook. Stir frequently. Add a little water if necessary. Salt and pepper to taste; add a little more sugar or vinegar if you prefer. Serve warm or cold.

—Sister Jean Evelyn
A Month of Dinner Menus, 1982

Salad Meal

This recipe comes from WSAI radio's "Wonder Kitchen," hosted by Edna Hutton, a talented homemaker and performer during the early 1950s. (The current station programmer claims to have no personal knowledge of that decade.)

Yield: 6 servings

1 cup lima beans, cooked
2 cups cooked and cubed potatoes
½ cup chopped celery
⅓ cup shredded carrots
⅓ cup cooked and cubed beets
4 hard-cooked eggs, chopped

½ cup chopped green onions
Salt and pepper to taste
2 cups French dressing, divided
Lettuce for garnish
6 to 12 tomato slices

Combine the beans, potatoes, celery, carrots, beets, eggs, and green onions and season with salt and pepper. Add one cup of the French dressing, mix well, and let marinate for one hour before serving. Arrange lettuce on six salad plates and place one or two slices of tomato on each. Mix the remaining dressing with the vegetables and place a mound on each plate. Serve with meat sandwiches.

Vinegar Cole Slaw

From the Dutch word *kool* for cabbage and *sla* for salad, these combinations are sometimes called Cold Slaw.

Yield: about 6 servings

1 medium head cabbage, shredded
1 small onion, shredded or chopped fine
1 green pepper, chopped
½ to ¾ cup chopped celery

1 teaspoon salt
1 teaspoon mustard seed
1 cup sugar
⅓ cup white vinegar or cider vinegar

Mix together the cabbage, onion, pepper, and celery. Stir the other ingredients into the slaw, adding the vinegar last so as not to sour the cabbage. Let stand to blend. Serve at room temperature or chilled.

—Rachel Griffin

Heavenly Hash

This title has been bestowed upon variant recipes through the last sixty years. In the twenties it appeared as a pickle relish, in the forties as a meat hash; this fruity formula is the latest rendition.

Yield: 5 cups

1 cup sour cream
1 11-ounce can mandarin oranges, drained
1 12-ounce can pineapple chunks, drained

1 cup miniature marshmallows (optional)
1 cup coconut
1 tablespoon sherry

Mix all of the ingredients together. Serve as a salad or a dessert.

—Peg Laux
Madisonville

Sour Cream Cucumber Salad

No summer picnic would be complete without crisp cucumbers in one dish or another. This is a particularly fine old recipe, using the traditional method of salting the cucumbers first. Although nutritionists claim salting removes many of the vitamins from the vegetable, it was done to remove some of the water and make the cucumber softer and more responsive to the seasonings.

Yield: 4 to 6 servings

2 medium cucumbers
1 medium onion
2 heaping tablespoons salt

2 bottle caps vinegar
¼ pint sour cream
Paprika for garnish

Slice the cucumbers and onion thinly. Place them in a bowl and sprinkle the salt on top. Cover with water and refrigerate overnight or at least three hours. Drain off all the water. Rinse and drain again. Add the vinegar to the sour cream and mix it through the vegetables thoroughly. Garnish with a light sprinkling of paprika.

—Ann Kohl
Madisonville

Hot German Potato Salad

This easy version of German potato salad is thickened with flour instead of egg to eliminate the possibility of curdling. It is shared by an Irish cook nicknamed Flynn because, as a child, she was always late for supper.

"Bridget O'Flynn, where have you been?
This is a fine time for you to come in..."

Yield: 6 servings

½ pound bacon
⅓ cup vinegar plus water to make
   ½ cup
1 to 2 teaspoons flour
1 teaspoon sugar

¼ teaspoon pepper
1 teaspoon salt
5 cups chopped cooked potatoes
½ cup chopped onion

Cut bacon into small pieces and cook until crisp. Combine ⅓ cup of the bacon drippings with the next five ingredients. Heat and stir until thickened. Add the potatoes, onion, and bacon. Toss and heat thoroughly.

—Matilda Bridget Daniels

Hyde Park Center Holiday Mold

Yield: 10 to 12 servings

2 cups hot (not boiling) water
1 6-ounce package strawberry-
   flavored jello
1 16-ounce can crushed pineapple,
   drained
1 16-ounce can whole cranberry

sauce
1 16-ounce can jellied cranberry
   sauce
1 10-ounce package frozen
   strawberries

Dissolve the jello in the water. Add the remaining ingredients and stir well to mix. Pour into a lightly greased mold and refrigerate overnight or longer.

—*Bake, Simmer 'n Stew*, 1981

Withrow High School. This twenty-four-acre campus located on Madison Road in Hyde Park was once a part of the estate of Andrew Erkenbrecker, founder of the Cincinnati Zoo. Construction on the buildings of Colonial Revival style was completed in 1919. In front of the school stands a majestic 114-foot clock tower, with dials facing in four directions. Nearby is a brick-and-concrete footbridge spanning a small ravine. This bridge is a fond memory of every Withrow student and graduate. Reconstruction on the bridge was completed in 1981, with funds raised by many wonderful and caring people. Drawing by Geneva South

46

Creamy Cole Slaw

This exceedingly popular slaw is served at picnics, with winter meals, and on barbecue sandwiches. This unusual rendition is made with beer which adds a piquant taste.

Yield: 6 servings

1 medium head of cabbage	1 teaspoon salt
1 green pepper	¼ teaspoon pepper
2 tablespoons celery seed	1 cup mayonnaise
1 teaspoon finely chopped onion	½ cup beer

Shred the cabbage and green pepper. Place in a large bowl and add the seasonings. Thin the mayonnaise with beer, add to cabbage, and toss well.

—The Hudepohl Brewing Company

Deviled Eggs

Few serious cooks would be without their special deviled egg serving plate, probably purchased at Ray Bachman's famous "Glass Barn" on Reading Road. Fifty-two years ago Ray uttered the magic words "Open Sesame!" and the barn doors opened to public display the largest selection of glassware "seconds" in the Midwest. The merchandise ranges from the sublime to the ridiculous but is most often inexpensive. No smart cook dares buy a piece of retail servingware without first checking with the always changing selection at the Glass Barn.

Yield: 2 dozen egg halves

1 dozen large eggs, hard-cooked	Dash Worcestershire sauce
3 to 4 tablespoons mayonnaise	Dash hot sauce
2 tablespoons sweet pickle relish	Salt and pepper to taste
½ teaspoon mustard	Paprika for garnish

Carefully peel the eggs and slice each lengthwise into halves. Remove the yolks from the whites and place the yolks in a small bowl. Mash the yolks slightly with a fork. Add all of the other ingredients except the paprika and mix. Adjust the ingredients according to personal taste. Stuff the egg whites so that the mixture mounds. Leave a fork imprint on each egg. Place in the deviled egg dish and sprinkle each lightly with paprika.

—Donna Marsh
Reading

Poppyseed Salad Dressing

Once sold at Findlay Market, bulk poppyseeds, a staple of European cooking, are now available at the Cincinnati Food Co-op on Hamilton Avenue in Northside. In its tenth year of existence, the diversified storefront has every intention of reserving a place for itself in this city's history.

Yield: 2 cups

½ cup vinegar 1 teaspoon lemon juice
½ cup honey 1 teaspoon dry mustard
1 cup salad oil 2 tablespoons poppyseeds
1 tablespoon chopped onion Salt to taste

Place in the blender in the order given and process about one minute. Note: This dressing is exquisite on spinach salad.

Ann Holiday

As far back as 1900 The Cincinnati Gas and Electric Company, then known as The Cincinnati Gas Light and Coke Company, offered cooking aids and appliance and lighting information to their customers.

On July 30, 1951 the *Times-Star* announced the introduction of Ann Holiday. This was to be the trade name for the many services The Gas and Electric Company offered to the homemakers of the community.

Ann Holiday's home base was at Fourth and Main Streets on the mezzanine floor, which was called Holiday Center because she helped find ways to make a "holiday" out of homemaking. She could also be found in high school and university home economics classes; at various women's organizations; at the annual Food Show in Cincinnati; at county and state fairs; and at home shows throughout the service area.

Holiday Center was a busy place—bursting with activity. Customers phoned Ann Holiday to request recipes, cooking tips, menus, and appliance and lighting information. Many times customers would visit Holiday Center with their blueprints seeking Ann Holiday's advice on kitchen planning and lighting and wiring layouts.

48

At the height of her popularity, there were twenty-eight women qualified to use the name of Ann Holiday. Fourteen were college-trained home economists to help with appliance and food information, and fourteen were college-trained lighting advisors helping homemakers achieve proper and attractive lighting.

However, in 1973, due to the nationwide decrease in promotional activities of the public utilities, the Ann Holiday and Home Service program was one of the functions which was discontinued. After twenty-two years of serving the homemakers of Cincinnati, Ann Holiday recipes still exist in many area homemakers' recipe files.

Quick Tomato Dressing

A unique Ann Holiday suggestion for salads was to toss the greens and dressing together in a plastic bag so the dressing was evenly distributed through the salad. Plan on one cup of dressing for each pound of greens.

Yield: 2 cups

½ cup salad oil
½ cup vinegar
½ cup sugar
½ cup tomato soup
½ teaspoon salt

½ teaspoon pepper
½ teaspoon paprika
½ teaspoon dry mustard
½ teaspoon Worcestershire sauce

Combine all of the ingredients in a blender container. Process for 30 seconds.

Note: Substitute chili sauce for the tomato soup for a "secret" salad dressing served in several local taverns.

Cooked Salad Dressing

An old-fashioned dressing for potato salad, cole slaw, or macaroni salads, this rich recipe is also good on tossed salad or the thoroughly modern layered salad.

Yield: 1 pint

½ cup sugar
1 tablespoon flour
1 teaspoon vinegar mustard
1 egg, well-beaten

½ cup milk
¼ cup hot water
½ cup vinegar
½ teaspoon salt

Mix all the ingredients well with a fork or wire whisk. Bring to a boil in a saucepan and boil, stirring constantly, for one minute. Serve hot on potato salads or other hot salad, or refrigerate and serve cold on cold salads.

—Sena Jones Ward

Soups and Chilies

Turtle Soup

circa 1918

After being coaxed to grasp at a stick, the turtle's head was chopped off. The body was removed from the shell with a sharp knife, and the entrails taken out. Some soaked the turtle overnight in cold salt water before using. Turtle meat could be cut up, dipped in flour and fried, or made into soup. It tasted somewhat like pheasant or chicken dark meat but had a firmer texture.

1 fresh turtle
1 small measure turnips
2 bunches of carrots, 3 if small
3 pounds onions
2 pounds tomatoes (boil before using)

½ box allspice
2 lemons
1 quart of cider or wine
6 hard-cooked eggs

Run the vegetables through a meat grinder. Make three cups flour browned and add when almost done. Put meat in water in another pot. When done take out and see that all bones are out, then run through a meat grinder. Put back into pot with items above, keep stirring until done and add salt and pepper to your own taste.

—Lizzie Pathe

Hilvers Mock Turtle Soup

For over fifty years Hilvers Catering has served at weddings, picnics, and other joyful occasions. Among their specialties is homebaked ham and potato salad, but this soup helped the family-owned company build its reputation. It is a troublesome recipe, not attempted since the death of Earl Hilvers, but his son found this original recipe in the files in his father's handwriting. There is a note at the bottom: *"We used three large six gallon pots to boil the calf heads, almost full of water. Two pots for the vegetables."*

Yield: 25 gallons soup

8 calves heads
2 beef tongues
10 pounds chuck meat
4 gallons celery, finely chopped
25 medium carrots, chopped
Onions, chopped
Mangoes (Remember, in
   Cincinnati this is a green
   pepper), chopped
Tomatoes, chopped
2 10-pound tins catchup
3 or 4 bags of mixed spices

1 quart table sauce
  (Worcestershire)
½ gallon vinegar
3 bottles chianti wine
3 dozen eggs, chopped fine
3 dozen eggs, sliced
12 lemons: squeeze juice, cut
   peel fine
12 lemons cubed
Parsley, finely chopped
10 cups brown flour, mixed
   in cold water

Remove the brains from the calves heads and set aside. Boil the calves heads, tongues and chuck meat in salt water. In another pot or two boil the celery, carrots, onions, mangoes, tomatoes, catchup and mixed spices until the vegetables are cooked. Grind all the meat from the calves heads mixture and add to the vegetables. Add water if necessary, salt and pepper to taste. Bring to a boil then simmer. Approximate boiling time for all should be four hours. Toward the end, add the Worcestershire sauce, vinegar, wine, eggs, lemons, parsley and brown flour. Boil the brains in salt water, chop, and add them too.

Original Mock Turtle Soup

This offering came from Middletown. It is an old but "practical" recipe for Mock Turtle Soup from the collection of Doc and Anna Schmidt of Cincinnati. It is transcribed just as it was written down.

1 calf head
1 extra set of brains
1 beef heart
1 cup mustard seed (yellow)
1 cup vinegar
1 mango
4 large carrots
3 large onions
3 lemons

1 bottle catsup
1 bottle worcestershire sauce
1 can tomato pulp (small)
10¢ mixed spice tied loose in a sack
½ teaspoon red pepper; if not hot enough add more salt to taste
2 good cups brown flour mixed with cold water

Cook the meat separate. Do not cook brains with meat. Leave brains in salt water ½ hour to take off the blood. Then skin and chop fine; add to the soup. Don't forget to strain the broth which the meat was cooked in so you don't get bones in the soup. Use a fine grind for all ingredients. Don't forget stirring the soup often. Slowly add the brown flour and water about ½ hour before soup is finished. When soup is finished cut up 1 dozen hard boiled eggs cut fine.

—Rose Wroda
Middletown

Modern Mock Turtle Soup

There are two basic modern recipes, one made with brown flour and one made with gingersnaps. These soups became popular after river turtles were too scarce to eat and calves heads became impractical. Beef is used for these modern soups and the most authentically tasting cut to use would be the beef heart or a combination of heart and chuck.

Yield: approximately 4 quarts

2 beef bouillon cubes
2 quarts water
1 pound ground beef
1 cup brown flour mixed with a little
   cold water
1 large onion
1 whole lemon
1 10-ounce bottle ketchup

1 16-ounce can beef gravy
1 tablespoon A-1 sauce
2 tablespoons vinegar
1 tablespoon whole allspice, or
   pickling spice tied in a bag
Salt and pepper to taste
2 hard-cooked eggs, chopped fine

Place the beef bouillon cubes in the water, bring to a boil and stir to dissolve. Add the ground beef and stir until completely blended. Mix the brown flour with enough water to make a paste. Stir into beef mixture. Grind the onion and lemon or chop them and add to the soup. Add all of the other ingredients except the eggs, bring to a boil, and simmer at least two hours. Add the eggs in the last fifteen minutes of cooking. Serve piping hot with oyster crackers, lemon slices, and/or a jigger of sherry wine.

Note: Orba is a butcher at Kroger's. He and Ruth make this at home in large batches to can. It is at its best reheated.

—Orba and Ruth Burchett
Goshen

Easy Mock Turtle Soup

This is the sweetest and easiest of all the Mock Turtle Soup recipes.

Yield: approximately 3 quarts

1 pound ground beef
2 quarts water
1 whole lemon
2 carrots
1 onion
1 14-ounce bottle ketchup

2 tablespoons Worcestershire sauce
Salt and pepper to taste
1 tablespoon pickling spices tied
   in a bag
12 gingersnaps
3 hard-cooked eggs, chopped fine

Place the ground beef in the water and bring to a boil, stirring frequently, until completely broken up. Grind or chop up the lemon, carrots, and onion and add to the soup. Add the ketchup and spices and simmer at least two hours. After an hour, add the gingersnaps, and stir until well blended. During the final fifteen minutes add the eggs. Serve with oyster crackers, lemon slices, and/or a jigger of sherry wine.

—Bob Goggins and Aunt Agnes Leppert

Beer-Cheese Soup

This recent favorite is a staple in Wisconsin, known as much for its cheeses and beer as Cincinnati is for its pork and beer. Many people think Milwaukee and Cincinnati are architecturally similar. There, as well as in other northern places, our Queen City of the West is known as the "southernmost northern city."

¼ cup butter or margarine
½ cup chopped celery
½ cup chopped carrots
½ cup chopped onion
½ cup chopped green peppers
1 garlic clove, chopped fine
6 tablespoons white or whole wheat
   flour
½ teaspoon dry mustard
6 cups chicken broth
¼ teaspoon hot sauce
1½ cups Cheddar cheese (about
   6 ounces), grated
1 12-ounce bottle beer or ale
Salt to taste

Melt the butter and add the vegetables and garlic. Sauté until tender but not browned. Blend in the flour and mustard. Gradually stir in the broth and cook until slightly thickened. Add the hot sauce and cheese and cook, stirring constantly, until well blended. Do not boil. Take off the heat. Just before serving add the beer and bring the soup to serving temperature without boiling. Salt to taste.

—Dot Thompson
Finneytown

56

Celery Soup

Yield: 8 to 10 servings

6 cups finely chopped celery
1½ cups finely chopped onion
1½ cups chopped potato
3 tablespoons finely chopped fresh
  parsley
1 or 2 garlic cloves, finely chopped

¾ cup (1½ sticks) unsalted butter
6 cups chicken broth
Salt and pepper to taste
1 cup heavy whipping cream
Chopped toasted almonds

In a large saucepan, sweat (sauté covered) the celery, onion, potato, parsley, and garlic in the butter. Cover with a buttered round of waxed paper (to prevent the moisture from escaping) and a lid, and cook over a low heat for 20 minutes or until vegetables are soft. Add the chicken broth, bring to a boil, and season to taste. Purée the mixture in batches in a blender or processor and transfer to another large pot. The recipe may be done ahead to this point. When ready to serve, beat the cream stiff. Heat soup till hot and serve with whipped cream and almonds.

—Betty Wester
Summit Gourmet Club

Game Soup

This recipe comes from a cookbook published for the seventy-fifth anniversary of Shillito's department store.

Two grouse or partridge, or, if you have neither, use a pair of rabbits; half a pound of lean ham; two medium sized onions, 1 pound of lean beef, fried bread; butter for frying; pepper, salt and two stalks of white celery cut into inch lengths; three quarts of water. Joint your game neatly; cut the ham and onions into small pieces and fry all in butter to a light brown. Put into a soup pot with the beef, cut into strips, and a little pepper. Pour on the water, heat slowly and stew gently for two hours. Take out the pieces of bird, and cover in a bowl. Cook the soup an hour longer; strain, cool; drop in the celery and simmer ten minutes. Pour upon fried bread in the tureen.

—Shillito's Every-Day Cook-Book and Encyclopedia
of Practical Recipes for Family Use *by Edna Neil, 1905*

Onion Soup

Yield: 6 servings

4 large onions
4 tablespoons butter or margarine
3 10½-ounce cans beef consommé
1½ cups beer

Salt and pepper to taste
Toast slices or hard French bread
Grated Parmesan cheese

Peel the onions and slice them thinly. Cook in the butter until soft and golden brown. Combine the consommé and beer and add to the onions. Simmer, covered, 45 minutes. Season to taste with salt and pepper. Pour into soup bowls. Top with toast slices and spinkle with cheese.

—The Hudepohl Brewing Company

Polish Easter Soup

(Barszcz)

The Kvapil name has been synonymous with the arts in Cincinnati for twenty-five years. A superlative director, Otto is likewise an outstanding cook. This family recipe is a traditional peasant dish served during the holiday season, passed down from Otto's mother who was born in Poland.

Yield: 4 to 6 servings

4 pork sausages, preferably kielbasa
   (1½ pounds)
2 tablespoons flour
1½ cups water

½ pint sour cream
4 hard-cooked eggs, chopped
1 tablespoon horseradish

Place the sausages in a skillet, pierce, cover, and cook on a low heat for one hour. Take the sausages out of the pan and set them aside. Cool the remaining broth in the refrigerator until the fat can be removed. Mix the flour with the water, add it to the broth, and heat until thickened. Cool slightly, then stir in the sour cream, eggs, and horseradish and whisk well. Cut the sausages in very thin pieces and add to the mixture. This soup can be served cold as a lunch with ham sandwiches, or warmed as the first course of the evening meal.

—Otto Kvapil, chairman of the
Theatre Department, Xavier University

The Taft Museum. Built in 1820 by Martin Baum who ran into financial crisis and never moved in, this home's history commenced as the Belmont School for Girls. Nicholas Longworth then purchased the home and was host several times to his good friend Abraham Lincoln. Millionaire forefather David Sinton bought the home from the Longworths, later encouraging his daughter Anna to marry into a "presidential" family. Anna married Charles Taft, brother of William Howard Taft. It was on the portico steps that William accepted his nomination for the presidency in 1908. The Taft Family deeded their home and magnificent art collection to the City of Cincinnati. Drawing by Edward Timothy Hurley

Children's Lunch Menu

Cincinnati Weenies and Chippie
(Wieners sliced like thick pennies
surrounding a mound of ketchup)

Acini de Pepe
(Good chicken broth with tiny pasta added,
found in Italian or specialty food stores.)

Banana
(The label from the banana should be stuck on the
child's nose when he goes back out to play.)

—The DuSablon/Alonzo family

Shaker Tomato Soup

Yield: Serves 6

1 small onion, chopped
½ cup finely chopped celery
2 tablespoons butter
1 10½-ounce can tomato soup
1 10½-ounce can water
1 teaspoon finely chopped parsley

1 tablespoon lemon juice
1 teaspoon sugar
Salt and pepper to taste
Whipped cream, unsweetened, for
  garnish
Parsley

Sauté the onion and celery in butter until the onion looks transparent. Add the tomato soup, water, parsley, lemon juice, sugar, salt, and pepper. Simmer five minutes. Celery will remain crisp. Top with unsweetened whipped cream and chopped parsley.

—Marjorie A. Frame

Beef Soup

This is nicer if you take two kinds of meat instead of one such as 5¢ beef bone and a 5¢ or 10¢ veal bone. Put into pot together and cover with cold water; boil until meat is tender. Take out, skin off most of fat; add enough boiling water to make quantity needed. Then add half head of cabbage, two or three onions, a carrot, two turnips, all cut up fine; also a sprig of parsley or celery. Pepper and salt to taste.
—Christian Women's Missionary Cookbook, 1921

Brussels Sprout Soup

This old English recipe came with the Cooper family's genealogy records. It has been updated from the country version, but none of its quality has been lost.

Yield: approximately 2 quarts

1½ pounds brussels sprouts	¼ teaspoon nutmeg
1 tablespoon butter	½ teaspoon brown sugar
3 pints chicken stock	1 tablespoon cornstarch
1 tablespoon lemon juice	Grated Parmesan cheese

Wash the sprouts and sauté them in butter for about five minutes. Choose 12 to 15 of the smallest and most attractive sprouts and set aside with the butter. Place the other sprouts in a soup pot with the chicken stock and simmer until tender. Place sprouts and some of the broth in the blender and process until uniformly coarse. Then place the processed sprouts back into the broth, along with the small whole sprouts and butter, lemon juice, nutmeg, and brown sugar. Mix the cornstarch with a little cold water and add that too. Simmer for five minutes and then serve hot, with a few whole sprouts in each bowl and a little grated cheese on top.
—Mary Jean Cooper
Pleasant Ridge

Crosley Field, home of the Cincinnati Reds 1912 to 1970. Redland Field was built at Findlay and Western avenues in the West End in 1912 with 30,000 seats. It was renamed Crosley Field when control of the club went to Powell Crosley, Jr. in 1934, a "temporary" investment which lasted almost a quarter of a century. The park endured floodwaters and face-liftings, but was eventually abandoned for the newer structure at the city's riverfront. Crosley Field is now only a memory, but a happy, heartfelt memory.

Hearnburner Chili

Named for a nineteenth century reporter, this chili is served at the Rookwood Pottery Restaurant. In this most incongruous establishment the huge kilns have been authentically preserved and form small, intimate rooms within the larger room for drinking and dining. Old photographs of the design and production of pottery grace the walls.

The original display room has been restored and contains an extensive collection of genuine Rookwood Pottery. Founded in 1880 by Maria Longworth Nichols, the building itself is now listed on the National Register of Historic Places.

Yield: 2 gallons

7½ pounds ground chuck
½ cup salad oil
5 cups chopped onion
1 medium stalk celery, chopped
5 cups chopped green pepper
9 medium tomatoes, chopped
3 beef bouillon cubes
2 cups water
2 bay leaves
½ teaspoon thyme

1¼ tablespoons garlic powder
2½ tablespoons salt
½ teaspoon black pepper
⅓ cup oregano
⅓ cumin
½ teaspoon chili peppers, crushed
1 tablespoon paprika
2 tablespoons Worcestershire sauce
1 quart tomato purée
2 cups kidney beans

Sauté the beef, drain fat, and set aside. In a large skillet sauté the onions, celery, and green pepper until tender. When the vegetables are soft, add the tomatoes and cook five minutes longer. In a large pot dissolve the beef bouillon cubes in the water, then add the vegetables and meat. Add seasonings, purée, and kidney beans and blend mixture thoroughly. Bring to a boil then simmer for at least two hours, longer if possible, so that the seasonings can blend flavors.

—Rookwood Pottery
Mt. Adams

Legend has it that Cincinnati, like Rome, was built on seven hills. However, there are considerably more hills than seven in the area, causing quite a lot of controversy about which ones were the "original seven." Mt. Adams, depicted here, is often a contender. Drawing by Betty Borchering

A Beatles Menu

The Beatles came to town twice, once in August of 1964 when they performed in Cincinnati Gardens and again in August of 1966 when they packed Crosley Field. For both concerts they occupied the Presidential Suite plus four additional rooms on the eighth floor of the distinctive Vernon Manor Hotel, owned at the time by Dr. Link. He recalls that they had either kidney pies or kippers and mackerel wtih eggs for breakfast. They were light eaters, snacking most often, although they ate nothing for three or four hours before concerts. Their favorite meal was fish and chips: filet of sole dipped in flour and egg, deep-fried in a margarine-butter-oil mixture, served with French fried shoestring potatoes.

They drank local beer, not too cold. Iced or hot, an orange pekoe/Ceylon tea brewed strong was their favorite drink. Lemon, cream, and sugar were provided as well as baking powder biscuits with butter, lots of jam, cookies, and crumpets.

They enjoyed our Mock Turtle Soup, a ground beef version homemade by the Vernon Manor. Another hotel dish popular with the British troupe was the chili.

Vernon Manor Chili

Yield: 6 servings

2 pounds top sirloin, freshly ground
2 green peppers, chopped
1 large onion, chopped
4 stalks celery, chopped
½ pound mushrooms, sliced
1 29-ounce can tomatoes

1 10-ounce can tomato soup
2 packages chili mix or
  3 tablespoons chili powder
2 15-ounce cans dark red kidney
  beans
1 to 2 quarts water

Brown the beef in an equal margarine-butter-oil mixture over a low heat. Add the green peppers, onion, celery, and mushrooms and sauté about five minutes, stirring frequently. Add all of the other ingredients and simmer until all the vegetables are tender, at least an hour. Add more water if necessary.

—Dr. Joseph Link, Jr.
Tudor Lodge

Cincinnati Chili

The first chili parlor opened its doors next to the Empress Burlesque (later named the Gaiety) in downtown Cincinnati in 1922, naming itself The Empress Chili Parlor. This establishment was owned by Greek Tom Kiradjieff who banked on the city sharing his taste for the unusual blend of spices. The rest is history. The original recipe which has always been mixed secretly at home, was never revealed. Yet chili restaurants sprang up all over town, including Skyline and Gold Star. Local chili aficionados developed preferences for their favorites. Al Heitz, a Camp Washington devotee, liked the old recipe best because it left his lips numb; old timers say that the chilies have indeed "cooled off" through the years. Inevitably, various chili recipes were published in homemade cookbooks. Recently, a packaged Cincinnati Chili Mix has appeared on supermarket shelves. Whether the chili is hot or not, Cincinnati prides itself on being a true chili capital.

Yield: 8 to 10 servings

2 to 3 pounds ground beef	2 teaspoons cinnamon
1 quart cold water	1 teaspoon allspice
1 6-ounce can tomato paste	2 cayenne peppers (more to taste)
2 large onions, chopped (about 1½ cups)	1½ tablespoons unsweetened cocoa
	Salt and pepper to taste
1½ tablespoons vinegar	1½ pounds cooked spaghetti
1 teaspoon Worcestershire sauce	1 pound Cheddar cheese, grated
1 garlic clove, chopped fine	1 box oyster crackers
2 tablespoons chili powder	1 16-ounce can kidney beans
5 bay leaves	1 onion, chopped fine (optional)

Crumble the raw ground beef into the water. Add all of the ingredients except the spaghetti, cheese, crackers, beans, and onions and bring to a boil. Stir well, breaking all the meat up before it cooks. Cover and simmer two or more hours, stirring occasionally.

The proper way to serve this chili is over spaghetti on an oval dish. (There should be a piece of pepper for every serving for absolute authenticity.) For a "3-Way," top it off with a pile of grated cheese with a dish of crackers on the side. To make a "4-Way," add a spoonful of onions before the cheese is placed on top. For a "5-Way," add beans in addition to onions and cheese. (See Coney Islands in the sandwich section.)

Note: Some prefer using whole spices tied in a bag: 5 bay leaves, 6 whole allspice, 4 red pepper.

> "...I have many good memories of my girlhood in Cincinnati...going to the beer garden with Aunt Hilda and Uncle Frank, my mother, and brother, to have roast beef, chili and orange pop, the lanterns swinging overhead while we sang along with the piano player; going to church on Easter, when everyone looked so beautiful in new dresses and suits; my days at the Welz Bakery when I was seven years old and my uncles let me wait on customers and make change and gave me my own dough and rolling pin and put my bread in the big oven; learning tricks on the trapeze which my cousin Carl had set up in the yard in back of the bakery; swimming in the creek in Trenton, and afterward eating Smitty's homemade ice cream; and in the evening, lingering over a nectar soda in the drugstore and then going back to the front porch and sitting in the swing, reading the funnies while listening to the radio. There were some happy times, all right."
>
> —Doris Day Her Own Story,
> Reprinted courtesy of William Morrow
> and Company, 1975

1st Prize Winning Firehouse Chili

Here it is, hot off the burner. Captain Weddington reveals for the first time anywhere his sought-after recipe which won first place in the 1982 Chili Contest at the Fireman's Museum in Cincinnati. Besides aroma, taste, and hotness, this chili was judged above its counterparts for its excellent aftertaste.

Yield: about 4 quarts

½ pound ground beef
½ pound ground beef heart
1 large onion, chopped
2 large hot green peppers, chopped
6 small red chili peppers
2 teaspoons cumin seed
2 teaspoons oregano
1 teaspoon cinnamon

2 whole bay leaves
1 8-ounce can jalapeño and tomato sauce
6 large fresh, peeled homegrown tomatoes or 1 28-ounce can tomatoes, chopped (Do not use hothouse tomatoes.)
1 8-ounce can tomato purée

Brown the meat, onion, and hot green peppers slowly in their own juices. Add the red peppers, cumin seed, oregano, cinnamon, bay leaves, and jalapeño and tomato sauce; stir well. Cook on low for one hour. Add the tomatoes and tomato purée, and simmer for an additional four hours, covered, adding water for desired thickness. Serve this chili as it is or over spaghetti.

—Capt. Jerry Weddington
New Burlington Fire Department

World's Hottest Chili

From two WLW radio personalities who were inspired by the hit television series, "That's Inedible."

Yield: 150 servings

2 16-ounce cans red kidney beans
1 pound lean ground beef
1 24-ounce can stewed tomatoes
8 tablespoons chili powder
10 medium onions, chopped

1 gallon Sohio no-lead Supreme
   (Lite, only 3 calories)
1 quart hot pepper sauce
½ canister Agent Orange

Combine all of the ingredients and sprinkle gingerly with half paprika, half nitroglycerine, and half plastic explosive. Add salt to taste. If desired for color add Red Dye #2. Bring to a rolling boil then simmer for 8 days or until the mixture has condensed to a black flab. Garnish with grated cheese. Serve and run.

—Gary Burbank and Bill Gable

Mad Dog Surrender Chili

It is rumored that this chili can bring a mad dog to its knees; therefore, the author of this recipe cautions the reader that an overdose can bring on a condition similar to the results of a frontal lobotomy.

Yield: 10 servings

1 pound pinto beans
¼ pound bacon, chopped
1 pound pork sausage
3 garlic cloves, crushed
1 large onion, chopped

2 stalks celery, chopped
1 green pepper, chopped
½ pound mushrooms, whole or
   chopped (optional)
1½ pounds beef chuck, cubed

68

Olive oil as needed	1 teaspoon Maggi or
4 16-ounce cans Italian tomatoes	Worcestershire sauce
1 bay leaf	4 level tablespoons chili powder
1 tablespoon basil	3 level tablespoons cumin
2 tablespoons parsley	1 teaspoon cayenne pepper
1 tablespoon oregano	1 8-ounce can tomato paste
1 tablespoon thyme	Tabasco sauce to taste

Boil the beans with the bacon for three minutes, then soak overnight in enough water to cover. The next morning drain, rinse, and set aside. Brown the sausage with the garlic, onion, celery, green pepper, and mushrooms. Drain off the fat. In a large Dutch oven heat the olive oil and brown the beef. Add the rinsed beans, bacon, and sausage mixture and stir well. Crush the tomatoes (use hands, not feet) and add with all the herbs and spices. Add water, if necessary, to barely cover. Simmer, covered, for two hours. Remove from heat and stir in the tomato paste. Taste and add the Tabasco sauce, no substitutes, according to proclivity for risk. Keep plenty of ice-cold Cincinnati beer at the ready.

Note: Louis recommends freezing this melange and bringing it on fishing trips.

—Louis A. Ginocchio, Jr.
Watch Hill

Frijoles con Queso

(Beans with Cheese)

From another Cincinnati company, Durkee Foods, once known as The Frank Tea and Spice Company, comes this recipe from a very old cookbook. Titled *The Wonderful World of Spices*, the small booklet claimed to be "A handy spice guide to make you become a seasoned seasoner."

Yield: 4 to 5 servings

2 slices bacon	½ teaspoon salt
½ medium onion, thinly sliced	¹⁄₁₆ teaspoon pepper
½ green pepper, chopped	1 tablespoon parsley
½ pound sharp Cheddar cheese, shredded	¼ teaspoon cumin
	2 tomatoes, chopped
1 tablespoon chili powder	½ cup tomato sauce
1 teaspoon oregano	1 16-ounce can kidney beans

Fry the bacon until crisp, drain, and crumble. Sauté the onions and green pepper in bacon fat until clear. Add the cheese and seasonings and heat, stirring constantly, until the cheese is melted. Add the tomatoes and tomato sauce and blend. Add the beans and cook slowly about five minutes or until beans are heated through, stirring constantly.

What are Spices?

The word "spice" is generally used today to cover the entire group of spices, seeds, herbs, and vegetable seasonings. True spices are parts of plants usually found in tropical zones. Seeds (mustard, caraway, poppy, etc.) are actually seeds or fruits of plants which grow in temperate or tropical zones. Herbs are leaves from temperate zone plants. And vegetable seasonings come from dehydrated ground vegetables such as onion or garlic. A blend is a mixture of two or more of these various seasoning agents.

—The Wonderful World of Spices
The Frank Tea and Spice Company

Sandwiches and Barbecues

The Fried Bologna Sandwich

For each sandwich toss a thick slice of bologna into a slightly greased skillet and brown on both sides at a medium temperature. Serve on bread with good mustard or ketchup. Add pickles if desired. If cheese is desired, brown bologna on only one side, causing the bologna to puff up in the center. Flip over, place a small slice of cheese in the "hole," and brown the downside on a low heat allowing the cheese to melt. Cover if necessary. If bologna is thinly sliced, place cheese between two bologna slices and brown both sides at medium heat as above. These pack well for lunches even though they may be cold when eaten.

Note: One more version of this sandwich is bologna and egg, with the egg between the bologna slices.

Sardine Sandwiches

The Cincinnati Public Schools Course of Study, *a study in homemaking, is contained in the archives of the Cincinnati Historical Society without cover, title page, date or author, but was probably published between 1900 and 1920. This recipe includes specific instructions for an old-fashioned but locally favorite lunch.*

"Any variety of bread 24 hours old may be used. Sometimes two varities are combined in the same sandwich. Let the bread, freed from crust, be cut into slices ⅛-inch thick . . . sandwiches are daintier if made small."

6 sardines
6 hard cooked egg yolks
3 tablespoons butter
Lemon juice
Paprica [sic]

Remove the skin and bone from the sardines. Mince fine with the yolks of eggs and the butter, season to taste with lemon juice and paprika. Spread crescent or other shaped pieces of bread with the paste and press together in pairs. Serve on a napkin; ornament with cress and slices of lemon.

CUTS OF MEAT.

Loins.—Best quality for roasts and steaks.
Rump, Tough.—Pot roast and steaks.
Round.—Fair steak, beef tea, beef loaf.
Top Sirloin.—Fair steak and pot roast.
Prime Ribs (six ribs.)—Fine roast.
Blade (three ribs.)—Fair roast.
Chuck (four ribs.)—Pot roast and stew.
Neck.—Stews and soups.
Brisket.—Corned and boiled.
Navel.—Corned and boiled.
Flank.—Steaks, boiled, stew.
Shoulder.—Soup.
Shin.—Soup.

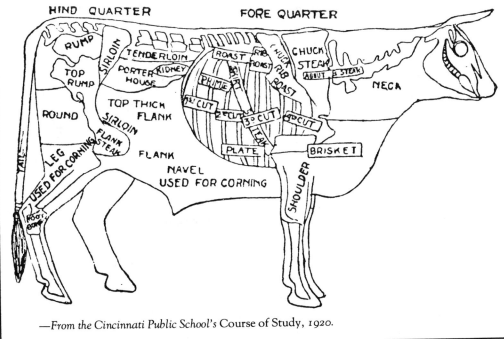

—From the Cincinnati Public School's Course of Study, 1920.

Limburger Cheese Sandwich

The Cincinnati Police Department has always had get-togethers through the seasons: picnics at Stricker's Grove, dances at Castle Farm, ballgames between districts, and Fraternal Order of Police meetings to name a few. One officer who did a lot of the cooking was Gene Simpkins, from the Community Assistance Department and police historian. He recalls that the fellows could really "pile it on," whether the meal was stew, barbecue, turkey roll sandwiches, or the perennial favorite: limburger cheese sandwiches with watermelon slices for dessert.

The limburger had to be the Moosewood Brand cake-type, not the smear type. A few slices were piled on a slice of Rubel's Rye Bread with a large slice of a Bermuda onion, ketchup or mustard to taste, and then another slice of rye.

This was accompanied by a big glass of "good ol' Cincinnati beer," or for non-drinkers, a bottle of pop.

The watermelons were sliced into wheels, then Gene sliced the center away from the rind, scraped off the seeds, then cut the circles into smaller pieces to be piled on deep, wax-coated paper plates.

After one such meal a fellow officer was heard to say, "Dammit Gene, if you were a woman I'd marry you."

Coney Islands

Whether you make Cincinnati Chili to eat as chili, with coneys made from the leftovers, or make the chili to eat expressly as coneys, you're in for one of the world's great sandwiches. This is not to be confused with the commonplace "chili dog" which uses any type of sloppy chili with beans.

For each coney you'll need a warm hot dog bun. Place a hot weiner inside, spoon on some Cincinnati Chili, then grated cheese (American, Cheddar, or colby), and chopped onions if desired. Some people spread a little mustard on the bun first, but that's a fairly recent innovation.

"Rookwood Pottery Menu"

McGuffeyburgher . . .
>   The basic fundamental best seller. Simple as ABC. (All Beef—with Character)

Farnyburgher . . .
>   An artistic delight painted with cheese as American as the Indian. You can canvass Cincinnati and find none better.

Inclineburgher . . .
>   No price is too steep for this mountainous burger capped with—what else? Yo de lady who?

Boss Coxburgher . . .
>   You'll vote twice for this big, powerful burgher hidden sinfully under tangy "bleu."

Stephen Fosterburgher . . .
>   Oh Susanna, now choose me if you please! I'm topped with lots of mushrooms and provolone cheese!

Erkenbrecherburgher . . .
>   As uplifting as a trip up the Incline on the Zoo-Eden street car to the home of wild boar and mountain goat.

Krogerburgher . . .
>   This one takes you from the meat counter through the produce department. Barney would have been proud of it.

Shillitoburgher . . .
>   What a treat you have in store when you shop around our toppings department and choose any three you like.

Coney Island. James H. Parker's apple orchard and picnic grove in California magically became Ohio Grove, "Coney Island of the West," June 21, 1886. It was advertised as "the most beautiful all-day summer resort in America" and boasted electric lighting. Soon it was known simply as Coney Island. Although accessible by boat along the Ohio River, the park was also vulnerable on this account. The aftermath of seasonal floods often caused workers to spend day and night hosing down rides and shoveling acres of mud out of Sunlight Pool, the world's largest circulating swimming hole. Until it closed in 1971, it afforded generations of Cincinnatians exciting and romantic memories. Drawing by Geneva South

The Hoagie Sandwich

It is amazing that very few cities offer hoagies cooked properly! They are usually sold cold, and if you request a hot sandwich it is warmed in a microwave. Cincinnatians prefer their hoagies hot and crusty on the outside, moist and steamy inside.

For each sandwich, start with a large hard roll. Slice it lengthwise and butter both sides lightly. Then build the sandwich, beginning with 3 or 4 slices of salami, 2 slices minced ham, 3 slices of Provolone cheese, 3 or 4 slices of mortadella if desired, and maybe some Swiss cheese too.

76

Vegetables may be placed on the sandwich before or after baking: a mound of shredded lettuce, 3 thin slices tomato, and 3 thin slices sweet onion, broken into rings. Sprinkle Italian dressing generously over the sandwich, pop on the top, wrap it in aluminum foil, and bake in the oven at 450 degrees F. for 15 to 30 minutes, depending on the size of the creation. Cut in half to serve. Dagwood would be proud.

Bacon and Egg Sandwich

This was a favorite sandwich among Catholic children who fasted overnight and brown-bagged their breakfast to eat at their desks after morning mass.

For each sandwich fry two slices of bacon. Remove. Add an egg and fry slowly, piercing the yolk as soon as the white begins to set. Flip once. Place both warm bacon and egg between two slices of bread and wrap with two thicknesses of waxed paper. Keep on the stove until ready to leave. Commuters nowadays enjoy this old standby, wrapping the sandwich in aluminum foil for munching in the car on the way to work.

Note: Many Cincinnatians enjoy ketchup on their eggs, and also on the bacon and egg sandwich.

Baked Bean Sandwich

For each sandwich use a thick slice of whole wheat or rye bread and cover end to end with cold home-baked beans. Add a slice of onion. This very old sandwich is served open-faced.

Heidi Bread

For each sandwich place a slice of bread, preferably whole wheat, under the broiler. When toasted, remove and place a slice of cow or goat cheese on the untoasted side. Return to the broiler and toast until the cheese is bubbly and slightly browned. If you have small children, they will enjoy sitting on the floor near the broiler to keep watch over the toasty morsels. Serve open-faced.

Wieners, Metts, n' Brats

Wieners are usually made of a mildly seasoned pork, mettwürsts from a more highly seasoned blend, and bratwursts from veal. They are uniform in size and precooked these days, a far cry from the strings that hung in the old butcher shops. Yet many Cincinnati butchers still make their own sausages. If precooked these juicy links can be heated in water, but they are best simmered slowly in broth or beer. The uncooked variety requires cooking for 45 minutes to an hour. Both types are delicious grilled outdoors until they are bursting with flavor. For each sandwich you'll want a good quality bun, perhaps with poppyseeds, and a selection of mustards; garnish with dill pickles and/or sauerkraut.

In a local magazine titled "Peebles Every Month," published from approximately 1900 to 1910 by the Joseph Peebles and Sons Grocers downtown and at Peebles Corner, the following sausages were listed for holiday enjoyment in 1901: braunschweiger, cervelatwurst, braunschweiger trufflewurst, ganseleberttrufflewurst, holsteiner bauernwurst, karlstader hams cured in salted milk, westphalische, schinken, and wild boar.

St. Stephen's Church Summer Festival Pork Barbecue

Yield: 3 dozen sandwiches

2 fresh pork Boston butts (3 pounds each)
2 10-ounce bottles Brooks ketchup
1 5-ounce bottle Worcestershire sauce
3 tablespoons brown sugar
3 teaspoons finely chopped parsley

The day before place the butts in a 350 degree F. oven with 2 cups of water, cover, and roast until well done. After the butts are done, cool and place both meat and juices in the refrigerator overnight. The next day, remove all hard grease and discard. Cut the pork in about 3 or 4 chunks, small enough to make very thin slices about 2 inches long and 1½ inches in width. Place the cooking juices in a pot, add the ketchup, Worcestershire sauce, sugar, and parsley. Put in the meat and add water, if necessary, to cover. Stir to mix all of the ingredients completely. Bring to a boil, and then simmer for 30 minutes or longer. Serve on buns with creamy cole slaw.

Note: Some people make this recipe using cooked, shredded pork roast, or a combination of pork, beef, and Boston butts.

—Juanita and Mike Pape

St. Rita School for the Deaf
Summer Festival Barbecue

Yield: 1 dozen sandwiches

2 pounds shredded cooked beef
   (such as roast leftovers)
1 green pepper, chopped
1 large onion, chopped

½ cup sweet pickle relish
½ teaspoon Accent
2 cups barbecue sauce

Mix the ingredients thoroughly. Bake in the oven at 350 degrees F. for approximately 45 minutes, or until the barbecue is firm and not soupy. Some may pefer to cook it in a saucepan on top of the stove. Serve on buns with creamy cole slaw, if available.

Note: This barbecue can be frozen; add a little more barbecue sauce and water when reheating.

—Gloria Rohrkasse and Opal Thompson

St. Rose Church
Summer Festival and Bingo Barbecue

Yield: 2 dozen sandwiches

2½ pounds lean ground beef
5 medium onions, chopped
1 10-ounce bottle ketchup
½ bottle Worcestershire sauce
   (5-ounce bottle)

5 tablespoons vinegar
5 tablespoons lemon juice
2½ tablespoons sugar
1½ teaspoons salt

Brown the ground beef slowly in a skillet, stirring frequently. Set aside. Cook the remainder of the ingredients about 15 minutes or until the onions are done. Add to the ground beef and simmer for 10 minutes or longer. Serve on a bun with your favorite cole slaw.

—Rose Litkenhaus

Main Dishes

Ohio River Baked Chicken

This primitive and amusing recipe dates back to the shantyboat days. Shantyboaters were river "gypsies" who lived on their houseboats, docking here and there as the mood suited them. They were customarily blamed, rightly or wrongly, for the disappearance of chickens and garden vegetables in low-lying neighborhoods.

Borrow a chicken. Take it down to the riverbank and build a good fire. Chop off the head, feet and remove innards. Do not remove feathers. While the fire takes hold and turns into burning embers, cover the chicken, feathers and all with a thick coating of mud. Sit the chicken directly upon the embers. Turn frequently with the hands being careful not to get burned. After an hour or two the chicken will be baked. Remove the baked mud along with the feathers. Sit down on a comfortable log and enjoy your meal. Potatoes and onions can be added to the coals in the same way, or without the mud if you're careful not to let them burn.

—Edgar Maxwell, lifelong resident of the Columbia-Tusculum Historic District, established 1788

City Chicken

It is believed this is strictly a Cincinnati recipe that came about because "some butcher probably had a pile of pork and veal scraps leftover one day," according to Russ Gibbs, Findlay Market's "oldest" proprietor with forty years at Butter and Egg Stand #28. City chickens are available ready-made at most of the meat stands, which number over half of the thirty-two stands inside the market building.

Yield: 2 to 3 servings

6 wooden skewers
1 pound lean pork
½ pound veal
½ cup flour

¼ cup cornmeal
Salt and pepper to taste
Frying oil

82

Cut the meat into bite-sized cubes. Thread the pork and veal onto the wooden skewers, two pieces of pork and one of veal, until all the meat is gone and each skewer has an equal amount. Place the flour, cornmeal, and seasonings into a bag and toss in the city chickens. Shake until the meat is well covered with the mixture. Fry at a medium heat, turning occasionally, until browned on all sides. This should take approximately 20 to 30 minutes so that the pork will be cooked through. Drain on absorbent paper. Afterwards, wash the skewers and use them again.

Note: The city chicken can be floured and dipped in an egg batter if so desired. Of course, Russ recommends this alternative.

Stewed Chicken and Homemade Noodles

In days gone by it was not unusual to bring the fat stewing chicken home from the butcher and find within it a string of uncompleted "egglets." These dainty yolk-type morsels floated on top of the simmering pot and were a special treat for whoever was lucky enough to spoon them onto their plate.

Yield: 6 to 8 servings

Chicken

1 fat stewing hen (5 to 6 pounds) plus giblets	1 small onion, halved
1 carrot, halved	1 stalk celery with leaves, halved
	1 teaspoon parsley

Noodles

2 eggs	Salt and pepper to taste
2 cups white flour (or half whole wheat)	2 to 3 tablespoons cornstarch (optional)

Cut the hen into enough pieces to lay in the bottom of your pot. Add the neck and giblets. Add the carrot, onion, celery, and parsley. Cover with cold water, bring to a boil, and simmer covered until the bird is tender, from 2 to 3 hours. While the chicken is stewing, make the noodles. In a small bowl beat the eggs until lemon colored. Beat in the flour with a fork, adding salt and pepper, until the dough forms a ball. Divide dough in half. Roll out on a liberally floured area until the dough is approximately ⅛-inch. Set in the sun or in a warm place to dry. Turn frequently, lightly flouring the up side. When the dough begins to dry but before it becomes brittle cut into ¼-inch wide noodles. Separate strips and set aside until just

83

before serving time. When the chicken is tender, remove and discard the vegetables. Bone the chicken, but leave the meat in large pieces and set aside, keeping warm. If desired the wings and legs may be left intact. About 15 minutes before serving time bring the pot once again to a boil and add the noodles. Boil ten minutes, uncovered. This should thicken the broth somewhat, but for a good, thick potmeal, add the cornstarch mixed with about ¼ cup of cold water. Simmer until thick, stirring constantly. Salt and pepper to taste. To serve, put the chicken back into the pot or bring to the table in a large heatproof bowl. A plate of stewed chicken, mashed potatoes, noodles, and green vegetable all covered with the thick, rich gravy is old-fashioned, sumptuous eating beyond words.

—Bernadette Martin
Mt. Washington

Crisco's Super-Crisp Country Fried Chicken

Yield: 4 servings

½ cup milk
1 egg
1 cup flour
2 teaspoons garlic salt
2 teaspoons MSG

1 teaspoon paprika
1 teaspoon black pepper
¼ teaspoon poultry seasoning
1 frying chicken, cut up
Crisco

Blend the milk and egg. Combine the flour and seasonings in a plastic or paper bag. Shake chicken in the seasoned flour. Dip chicken pieces in the milk-egg mixture. Shake chicken a second time in seasoning mixture to coat thoroughly and evenly. Shallow or deep fry in hot Crisco.

—from *Good Cooking Made Easy*, 1978
Reprinted courtesy of
The Procter & Gamble Company

Milk Gravy

Serve this rich gravy with roasts, chops, fried chicken, ham, pork sausage, grits, noodles, dumplings, or whatever. For each cup of gravy use two tablespoons butter, oil, or pan drippings. Add two tablespoons flour and stir until smooth. Then cook over low heat, stirring steadily, until it's all bubbly and brown. Add one cup of liquid, half meat juices, half milk. Take the pan off the heat to avoid lumps. Return pan to heat and stir until smooth and thickened. Dry instant milk may be added to the meat juices instead.

—Mary Rose Pitzer

Wray Jean's Chicken and Noodles

Known as the BBS to its friends in nine states, the Bob Braun Show celebrated fifteen years of success on WLW-T in 1982. Still as popular as ever, there is a waiting list of one year for the hundred seats available at the daily live variety-talk show. Cincinnatians have followed Bob's career from his early television and radio days through his courtship and marriage to Wray Jean, and their family's personal legacy to this city's history.

Yield: 6 servings

1 10½ can cream of mushroom soup
1 cup sour cream
Salt and pepper to taste
6 chicken breasts
12 ounces noodles

Mix the soup and sour cream together. Spread half of the mixture in a shallow baking pan. Salt and pepper the chicken and add it to the pan, meaty side up. Spoon on the remaining sour cream mix and bake uncovered for 1½ hours at 325 degrees F. During the last half hour of cooking boil the noodles according to package directions. Drain, stir them into the chicken and sauce and serve.

—Wray Jean Braun

Chicken Paprika

(Paprika Huhn)

2 young chickens, about 2½ pounds each
½ tablespoon salt
½ cup (1 stick) butter
1 large onion, chopped
2 teaspoons paprika
½ tablespoon flour
2 cups stock or bouillon
1 tablespoon heavy cream
1 cup thick sour cream
2 tablespoons chopped fresh dill

Rinse the chickens and pat dry. Cut in serving pieces and season with salt. Place in a covered bowl in the refrigerator for 30 minutes. Heat the butter in a deep pot of dutch oven until light brown. Add the onion and cook until transparent. Stir in the paprika and add the chicken. Cook slowly until pieces are golden, then cover and cook 30 minutes longer or until tender. Sprinkle with flour. Add stock and heavy cream. Stir. Cover and let boil 15 minutes. Remove chicken to warmed serving dish. Stir sour cream into pot and simmer 5 minutes. Pour over the chicken and sprinkle with dill.

—Dick Mohaupt
Grammer's Restaurant

Coq au Vin Blanc

This recipe comes from the Meiers Wine Cellar booklet "Isle St. George—Story of Great American Wines."

Yield: 8 servings

2 chickens
4 tablespoons butter, divided
2 tablespoons salad oil
1 large carrot, chopped
1 onion, chopped
Salt and pepper to taste
Pinch cloves
Sprig thyme
Sprig parsley
1 bay leaf

1 stalk celery, chopped
1 garlic clove, chopped fine
1 fifth of Isle St. George Chablis
2 tablespoons white flour
1 pound mushrooms
1 pound small white onions
Swiss cheese, grated or julienne, for garnish
Croutons for garnish

Quarter the chickens and sauté them in a heavy skillet until they are brown on all sides, using two of the tablespoons of butter and the oil. Remove the chicken and set aside; then sauté the carrots and onions. Transfer all to a heavy casserole, season with salt, pepper, cloves, thyme, parsley, bay leaf, celery, and garlic. Pour the Chablis over all and bring to a boil. Reduce the heat and simmer, covered, 45 minutes. While the chicken is cooking, sauté the mushrooms and onions in a small amount of butter. Cover, and cook in their own liquids over a very low heat until tender. Remove the chicken, place on a serving platter, and transfer to a hot oven. Make a roux of the remaining butter and flour; that is, mix it together well. Add to the liquids in the casserole, slowly, stirring constantly with a wire whip. Then strain and pour over the chicken. Top with some grated cheese, or narrow thin strips. Place under a broiler for a few minutes to brown. Garnish with the mushrooms and onions. Serve piping hot, garnish with heart-shaped croutons and have your guests wash down with goblets of chilled Isle St. George Chablis.

86

Chicken Mama Mia

"We cherish this recipe with infinite love and praise in the memory of our dear talented mother who prepared it for us in our early childhood. We can still recall the aroma of savory herbs that filled the kitchen as we watched her moving about, so graceful yet with a calm precision in her work. Eventually this chicken was featured as a specialty on our menu and relished by our patrons, some of the most generous and gifted people Cincinnati has ever known."

Yield: 2 to 3 servings

1 whole broiler (3 to 3½ pounds) cut in breasts, legs, and thighs *or* 6 halved chicken breasts
½ cup olive oil
3 tablespoons red wine
6 tablespoons white wine (Sauterne)
1 tablespoon lemon juice
4 2-inch strips lemon peel
2 garlic cloves, sliced
1 teaspoon thyme
½ teaspoon marjoram
½ teaspoon oregano
⅛ teaspoon sugar
4 tablespoons butter

Remove the skin from the breasts, legs, and thighs or have the butcher do it beforehand. Mix all of the remaining ingredients except the butter in a large bowl. Taste and adjust the seasonings. Arrange the chicken parts on a large tray or pan. Add salt and freshly ground pepper to your taste over each piece, turn, and repeat. Using a large spoon, pour the marinade over the chicken, tossing and coating thoroughly, allowing the herbs to adhere to the chicken. Place the chicken in the bowl, cover, and refrigerate overnight. At intervals toss the chicken pieces in the marinade. About an hour or so before serving, place a layer of heavy aluminum foil over the broiler plate and preheat the broiler for several minutes. Place the chicken under a medium heat broiler. After several minutes, baste with the marinade. Broil for 5 to 6 minutes, then turn the pieces, baste, and broil 5 more minutes. Continue basting and broiling until the chicken is browned and the edges are slightly charred. Preheat the oven to 300 degrees F. Remove the chicken from the broiler and place in a new pan. Spoon some of the marinade from the broiler over the chicken along with the butter. Cover tightly and place in the oven for about ten minutes. To serve, spoon the sauce over the chicken parts and garnish with parsley sprigs.

—Mary Valerio
Valerio's Restaurant

Quail and Peppers

A very pretty luncheon dish is made by broiling six quail a nice brown,
place on squares of buttered toast and lay on a large platter. Select six
smooth peppers, red, yellow and green, remove the contents, scrape and
wash well and fill with celery salad, place the peppers in among the quail,
and make a border of nasturtiums, selecting the yellow and green ones
with their leaves. This makes a very decorative dish.

—Mrs. Burton
School of Housekeeping Cookbook, 1900

Smothered Pheasant

In the fall many Cincinnatians "take to the hills" for some wild game
to add to the freezer: rabbits, venison, and gamebirds. Roast pheasant can
be dry if not cooked properly, a sad waste of an exquisitely flavored bird.

Yield: 2 servings

1 1-pound pheasant
¼ cup whole wheat or white flour
Salt and pepper to taste

4 tablespoons margarine
1 pint sour cream or milk gravy

Dry-pick, draw, and clean the pheasant with a damp piece of
cheesecloth, using as little water as possible. Cut the pheasant and blot the
pieces. Then combine the flour, 2½ teaspoons of the salt, and the pepper.
Place flour in a paper bag with the pieces of pheasant and shake the bag
until the pieces are well coated with the flour mixture. Melt the margarine
in a deep pan or skillet and brown the pheasant in it. Pour the sour cream
or gravy over the pheasant. Cover and bake at 250 degrees F. for two
hours, or until the pheasant is tender.

—Mary Rose Pitzer
Mt. Washington

Aunt Dee-dee's Turkey Gravy Hint: Cut giblets very small, mash some
liver pieces, add to drippings, and let gravy simmer a long time.

Music Hall. In 1873 the May Festival began, and the next year an "auditorium" was planned by Reuben Springer, John Shillito, and others. The fund-raising was successful, including donations of pennies, nickles, and dimes from school children. However, the high-Victorian Gothic, red brick building wasn't beautiful in everyone's eyes. One critic described it as "Sauerbraten Byzantine," a comment long since declared inappropriate. Drawing by Paul Blackwell, courtesy of Row House Gallery, Milford

Grammer's Hasenpfeffer

Grammer's Restaurant, the oldest German restaurant in Cincinnati, has been in continuous service since 1872. It is located in the historic Over-the-Rhine district, a short distance from downtown.

Yield: 4 servings

1 medium-sized rabbit (about 5 pounds)
White distilled vinegar, to cover
2 medium carrots, chopped
2 medium onions, chopped
1 small stalk celery, chopped

1 ounce whole mixed pickling spices
2 tablespoons salt
1 tablespoon pepper
3 garlic cloves
½ pound old-fashioned gingersnaps
2 ounces imported port wine

Cut the rabbit into six equal portions and place in a crock. Cover with vinegar, vegetables, spices, and garlic. Marinate for three days. Remove the rabbit and sauté to a golden brown. Place in a roasting pan; strain the vegetables from the marinade and pour over the rabbit. Add gingersnaps and wine. Cover and roast at 425 degrees F. for 1½ hours. For a real German feast, serve with potato pancakes or potato dumplings. Prosit!

Note: If a less sour flavor is desired, dilute the vinegar with water up to 50 percent.

—Dick Mohaupt, Manager

Wood Chuck

A quick, easy old standby, similar to Rarebit, this too is thought to be of English origin in spite of the noodles!

Yield: 10 to 12 servings

½ cup (1 stick) butter
1 green pepper, chopped
6 tablespoons flour
2 10-½ ounce cans tomato soup
2 cups milk
1 pound Cheddar cheese, grated

2 4-ounce cans mushrooms, drained
1 4-ounce jar pimentos, drained
1 dozen hard-cooked eggs, chopped
Chow mein noodles

Melt the butter in a large skillet and add the green pepper. Cook on a low heat until the pepper is soft. Add the flour and stir until smooth. Let bubble two or three minutes. Turn off the heat and stir in the tomato soup.

Gradually add the milk, and then heat until thickened. Turn off the heat and add the cheese of your choice. Stir in the mushrooms, pimentos, and eggs. Serve over chow mein noodles.

—Louise Hansen
Mt. Auburn

Liver n' Onions

Variety meats rate high among Cincinnatians. The trick is knowing how to cook them properly.

Yield: 6 servings

6 slices bacon
2 medium onions, sliced and
  separated into rings
¼ cup white flour
1 teaspoon salt

½ teaspoon paprika
¼ teaspoon pepper
1 pound calves liver (or other tender
  liver), sliced
⅓ cup vinegar (dilute if you like)

Cook the bacon in a large skillet until crisp; crumble and set aside. Add the onions to the drippings. Cook slowly, uncovered, until tender, stirring frequently. Remove the onions and set them aside. In a pie plate, thoroughly combine the flour, salt, paprika, and pepper. Coat the liver slices with the seasoned flour. Sauté the liver quickly in the same skillet, over a high heat, taking care not to overcook and toughen the meat. When the liver is still pink in the center, remove to a hot platter. Pour off excess fat from the skillet, add the vinegar, and stir well. Sprinkle the onions and crumbled bacon over the liver. Spoon the vinegar glaze over each serving.

—Dolores Daly
Hyde Park

Stupid people may eat, but shouldn't talk. Their mouths will do well enough as banks of deposit but not of issue.
—The Household Companion and
Family Receipt Book *by*
C. B. Unzicker, *1870*

The canal at Vine. Before it was drained, filled, and resurfaced, Central Parkway was the Miami Canal. It extended from Lockland to the Courthouse downtown with a depth of at least four feet. Directed toward the Ohio River, the canal was used for transportation, for boat harboring, and to turn industrial wheels. Canals were instrumental in tripling Cincinnati's population between 1820 and 1840. Note the streetcar in the upper left corner of the picture. Drawing by Edward Timothy Hurley

Elsie Firstos's Sauerbraten

Elsie Engler and Karl Firstos met and fell in love in Cincinnati, but didn't marry until they saved enough money to spend their honeymoon in their native Germany five years later. When they returned, they opened a lunchroom and bakery on Vine Street. Elsie stirred up the soup and served the sandwiches while Karl created dessert masterpieces including lily and violet confections. In 1980 Elsie was honored by *The Cincinnati Post* as one of the "Best Cooks in Town."

Yield: 16 to 24 servings

92

1 whole sirloin or rump roast, 8 to 12 pounds	1 to 2 quarts water
1 cup mixed pickling spices	Shortening for coating
1 onion, sliced	Salt and pepper to taste
1 lemon, thinly sliced	1 carrot
1 to 2 quarts white vinegar	1 stalk celery
	8 cups brown flour (see page 94)

Six days before serving, place the meat in a large crock and sprinkle with pickling spices. Place the onion and lemon around the roast. Pour one quart of the vinegar over the meat. Fill the empty bottle with water and pour that over the meat also. Press the meat down into the liquid. If the liquid does not cover, add equal parts of vinegar and water until it does. Cover the crock with clear wrap, placing a rubber band around it (or tie it) to keep it in place. Refrigerate. You may have to remove a rack to make this fit. Turn the meat every day.

When ready to roast, preheat the oven to 425 degrees F. Remove the meat from the marinade and dry it with a turkish towel. It will look grey. Rub the meat lightly with shortening, salt, and pepper. Grease the bottom of an enamel roasting pan and place the meat in it as well as the onion from the marinade, the carrot, and the celery. Roast uncovered for thirty minutes, on the bottom rack. Turn the vegetables during cooking so that they brown on all sides. Turn the roast browned side down; reduce heat to 350 degrees F. Roast covered one hour longer. Check for doneness by piercing the meat about one inch deep; if it draws blood it is not done. While the meat is roasting, strain the marinade into a large pot and discard the spices. Bring to a boil, simmer five minutes, and then set aside. When the roast is done remove it to a platter to cool. Add one cup of boiling water to the drippings. Stir and scrape well, getting up all of the brown from the pan. Strain into a large pot. Add one quart of the prepared marinade. Beginning with 6 cups of flour, in a bowl, mix the brown flour with cold water (using your hand) until a paste forms that is smooth and almost runny. Bring the drippings and marinade to a boil, adding the brown flour paste until the gravy is the thickness you prefer, stirring constantly. Salt and pepper to taste. Slice the cooled meat in ¼-inch slices diagonally. Place a ladle of gravy in the bottom of a large pan or casserole dish and cover the gravy with a layer of meat slices. Repeat layering until all the meat is sliced. Stir the scraps of meat that have fallen away into the remaining gravy to be served with späetzle or noodles.

Note: It is best to roast the meat the day before serving as this improves the taste considerably. Remove from the refrigerator several hours before reheating. Heat in the oven for 1½ hours at 325 degrees F., covered with foil. Check to make sure it is bubbling hot. Lift the meat occasionally with a spoon while heating to distribute the hot gravy from the edges.

Brown Flour

Spread 8 cups white flour evenly on a large cookie sheet with sides. Place on the bottom rack in a 350 degree F. oven. Stir gently every 15 minutes. The edges brown first, stir the browned flour toward the center. In about two hours the mixture should be a light chocolate color, evenly browned. If not, roast longer. Take care it does not burn. Do this well in advance as the whole house smells when you do it.

—Elsie Firstos
Westwood

Modern Sauerbraten

Modern Sauerbraten is a delectable dish in its own right. It is easier to make, using gingersnaps to thicken and flavor the gravy instead of brown flour.

Yield: 6 to 8 servings

1 beef roast (rump or round, 3 to 3½ pounds)	6 whole allspice
1 onion, sliced	4 bay leaves
1 carrot, sliced	1 teaspoon salt
1 stalk celery, chopped	2 cups apple cider vinegar or red wine vinegar
8 peppercorns	2 cups cold water
6 whole cloves	2 tablespoons salad oil

Gravy

3 tablespoons butter	2 cups marinade
3 tablespoons flour	6 gingersnaps
½ cup cold water	

Place the roast in a deep bowl. Add the rest of the ingredients except the oil. If there isn't enough liquid to cover the meat add more: half vinegar, half water. Cover and refrigerate for four days. On the fifth day remove the meat from the bowl, pat it dry with paper toweling and brown it on all sides in a heavy pot. Strain the marinade and add to the pot; bring it to a boil, then reduce the heat. Cover and simmer for 2 to 3 hours, or until the meat is fork tender.

94

To make the gravy: melt the butter in another pan, then stir in the flour and cook over a low heat about two minutes. Add the cold water and stir until smooth and thickened. Stir in the two cups of marinade and cook another few minutes. Toss the gingersnaps into the blender and process until they are completely crushed. Shake them into the gravy and cook, stirring constantly, until the mixture is smooth and thick. Salt to taste. Remove the meat from the pot and discard the remaining marinade. Slice the meat on a slant then place back into the pot, covering each layer of meat with gravy. Keep warm until serving time. Serve with späetzle, noodles, or dumplings with red cabbage on the side.

—Mary Krabacher
Cheviot

"The 'Cincinnati Dutch' are not necessarily German or Dutch, of course, never wear wooden shoes, and don't speak with a corny gutteral. It's more a state of mind than anything else. Such people generally avoid the flash and glitter of young moderns, support churches and building-and-loan associations by the score, save so much for rainy days they could buy a fleet of Arks for cash, favor a simple neighborhood tavern to an erotic cocktail lounge where the waitresses get chapped knees . . ."

—Dick Perry
Vas You Ever in Zinzinnati?, 1966

Beef Roulade

(Fleisch Rolle Den)

This is a German recipe. The name, loosely translated, means "roll-the-meat."

Yield: 2-4 servings

1 round steak, ½-inch thick	2 strips bacon, chopped
1 tablespoon German mustard	1 small onion, chopped
Salt and pepper to taste	¼ pound Swiss cheese

Bone the steak and cut off most of the fat. Spread the steak with mustard. Sprinkle with salt and pepper. Top with the bacon and onion, then cover with shredded or chopped cheese. Roll up like a jelly roll and tie. Slowly fry in a little fat, browning on all sides. Add enough water for gravy, then cover and simmer until tender, about 45 minutes.

—Gertrude Fisher
Oakley

95

Steak Diane

One of Cincinnati's hottest night spots is the historic Precinct, hangout for Bengal players and fans.

Yield: 2 servings

½ cup Marsala wine
1 teaspoon Dijon-type mustard
Touch of Worcestershire sauce
2 drops hot sauce
Dash bittersweet chocolate
20 medium mushrooms, sliced
½ tomato, chopped
1 shallot, chopped fine
½ teaspoon finely chopped garlic

2 tablespoons chopped fresh
  parsley
3 tablespoons butter
8 ounces beef tenderloin, halved
Salt and freshly ground pepper to
  taste
Brandy to taste
1 teaspoon chef's brown sauce

Mix together the wine, mustard, Worcestershire sauce, hot sauce, and chocolate in a medium sized bowl. Stir in the mushrooms, tomato, shallot, garlic, and parsley; refrigerate overnight. At serving time melt the butter in a small skillet. Add the steaks and sauté them for about 30 seconds on each side, flattening them slightly for medium well. Add salt and pepper. Pour a little brandy over them and flame. Put the flame out, then remove the steaks to a hot platter. Let the butter and brandy cook down some, add the mushrooms and sauce, and let the vegetables cook and the mixture reduce. Then add the brown sauce and reduce again. When the sauce is thick and ready, put the steaks back into the skillet and coat them well. Place the steaks on individual serving dishes and spoon the mushrooms and sauce over them.

Note: The secret to this recipe is not to let any one of the seasonings overpower the others. Beef may be added to marinade, if desired.

—Captain Jimmy Hussey
Precinct Restaurant

SINCE
1981

THE
PRECINCT

Good Food - Good Fun - Good Friends

The Precinct. One of Cincinnati's successful renovations, the Precinct Restaurant is housed within former Police Patrol House Number 6. The Romanesque-styled structure was designed and constructed by the Cincinnati firm of Samuel F. Hannaford and Sons in 1901, widely recognized for its works which include Music Hall, City Hall, and General Hospital.

Steak Pie

This is a Scottish recipe, from Mary Anne's grandmother Mary McNay Thomas. It was prepared in an "ashet," a square porcelain deep dish with a 2-inch lip for ease in sealing the pie crust. A funnel or a pie bird (crow) is placed in the center of the pie to allow steam to escape so that the crust doesn't get too soggy. Animals such as rabbits and chickens are also available as funnels in Scotland; meat pies are a staple in Great Britain.

Yield: 1 pie

Filling

3 pounds round steak
Salt, pepper, and flour to taste
1 medium onion, chopped

1 pound pork sausage links
1 small kidney (¾ pound)

Crust

2 cups flour
1 teaspoon salt

¾ cup shortening
5 to 7 tablespoons cold water

Pound the round steak with salt, pepper, and flour. Brown in hot oil. Cover with water and add the chopped onion. Cook at 350 degrees F. until tender. Be sure to save the juices for gravy. Puncture the links with a fork. Cover with water and cook over medium heat for about 10 to 15 minutes. Soak the kidney in salt water (1 tablespoon salt to 1 quart water) for approximately one hour. Drain and remove the skin and tubes. Cover with cold water and bring to a boil. Simmer for 20 minutes. Drain, then cut in slices, and remove any fat. Cut the round steak into serving size pieces. Place the steak, links, and kidney slices in a large ashet or 2½ quart casserole. Thicken the steak juices to a thin gravy consistency; then season and pour over meats.

To make the crust, sift the flour and salt together. Cut in the shortening with a pastry blender. Add water and toss with a fork until the mixture is moistened. On a lightly floured surface, roll to desired size. The pie crust should be a little thicker than a normal pie crust. Cover the ashet or casserole with the crust. Score the top and insert funnel in center to permit steam to escape. Bake one hour at 375 degrees F. If the crust is browning too fast, turn the oven back to 350 degrees F.

Note: Because of the length of time this recipe takes to prepare, you can prepare the meat a day in advance and the pie crust the day of baking.

—Mary Anne Will
Milford

98

Beefsteak Pudding

During the 1976 Bicentennial year, Cincinnatian Maey Schott sat down in her kitchen and copied out recipes that her grown family had enjoyed. She passed on to her children the "formulas" she inherited from as far back as her grandparents time. This recipe came from England. In days gone by it was an economical meal, flank steak being considered a "lower grade" piece of beef. The pudding was traditionally served with creamed lima beans and corn, plus a salad of lemon jello, walnuts, apples, and seeded red grapes.

Yield: 2 puddings

4 cups white flour
2 cups ground suet
1 teaspoon salt
2 tablespoons shortening
1½ to 1¾ cups warm water

3 flank steaks, cut in 1-inch squares
2 large onions, chopped
1 garlic clove, chopped fine
   (optional)

Rub the suet through the flour thoroughly. Add the salt and shortening. Mix well, like a pie dough. Add water, knead lightly. Roll out on a floured board. Cut the pastry to fit two bowls or pans with rims, leaving enough pastry for lids. Line the containers with the dough. Put in the meat, onion, and garlic. Add a little salt and pepper and sprinkle with flour to thicken into gravy as it cooks. Cover the meat mixture with boiling water. Moisten the side edges of the dough, add the covering dough, and seal. Place a dish towel over the pan and wrap a string around the container underneath the rim to hold the towel in place. Lift up the edges of the towel and tie them on top of the container. Immerse the pudding in boiling water. Cover loosely. Cook three to four hours, checking periodically to see that the water does not boil off. Add more if necessary.

Note: If by some miracle one pudding is left over, it may be frozen. Thaw completely and cook uncovered about one hour at 350 degrees F.

—Maey Schott
Western Hills

Italian Spaghetti

This recipe is shared with us by Mildred Cassinelli, sister of Margaret who was coordinator of the Our Lady of Mercy Hospital Candy Stripers' cookbook titled *Cooking Volunteer-ily*, published in 1967. The Cassinellis feel the secret to superb spaghetti sauce is the long, slow cooking.

Yield: 2 to 4 servings

4 tablespoons olive oil
1 onion, sliced and broken into rings
2 garlic cloves, chopped fine
1 green pepper, chopped
½ pound ground beef
4 anchovies
1 29-ounce can tomatoes

1 8-ounce can tomato paste
1 bay leaf
¼ teaspoon basil
¼ teaspoon thyme
½ cup red wine (or 2 tablespoons vinegar and a tablespoon of sugar)
Salt and pepper to taste

Make this spaghetti sauce in a large, deep aluminum or stainless steel skillet or dutch oven. Iron and tomatoes just don't get along. Heat the olive oil in the pan, add the onion, green pepper, and garlic. Sauté until the vegetables are soft. Add the ground beef, breaking it into shreds with a fork. Saute until it is browned through. Wipe dry the anchovy filets and mash them into a paste with a fork. Mix into the meat. The anchovy flavor won't be pronounced in the final result, but the tiny fish give wonderfully subtle overtones. Now the tomatoes go in, blend them first if desired. Mix thoroughy and add the herbs. Add the wine (or vinegar and sugar); then salt and pepper to taste. Place a cover on the pan, set over a low flame and simmer for three hours. Stir occasionally and see that the liquid isn't cooking away. If it is, add a little water. The sauce should be thick and rich. It's this long cooking that takes the bitter edge off tomatoes.

—Margaret Cassinelli

"Findlay Market has changed a lot in the 21 years I've been in business here, and then again it hasn't changed at all. You can get anything you want here...meats, fish, cheeses, fresh produce, farm eggs, tub butter...but some of the old recipes are disappearing. Kids don't like some things, so mothers don't serve it. They should let the kids develop a taste. You learn to eat at home."

—Mary Davis of M. Davis Meats
Findlay Market, Stand #11

Spaghetti and Breadcrumbs

In many Italian homes a basket is kept on top of the refrigerator for leftover pieces of bread to dry. The pieces are grated or crumbled in the blender or food processor for use in making meatballs and other dishes including the following very old recipe.

Spaghetti
Seasoned breadcrumbs to taste
Olive oil to taste

Oregano to taste
Wedge Romano cheese

Boil the spaghetti according to package directions. While the spaghetti is cooking, sauté the breadcrumbs in the olive oil. When the spaghetti is finished, drain and toss with olive oil and a little oregano; salt and pepper to taste. Serve the spaghetti on a warmed dish with the sautéed breadcrumbs on top. Grate some Romano cheese over this.

Note: If you prefer sauce, warm a can of tomato sauce and pour over the spaghetti before the crumbs and cheese. Another variation is adding a drained can of clams, with or without the sauce.

—Grandma Teresa Sorrentino
Madisonville

A Hearty, Warming Winter Meal

This typical meal, representative of the "substantial" cooking of Cincinnatians is shared with us by Virginia Schoettelkotte, cousin of the illustrious television newscaster Al Schottelkotte whose father, according to family members, "shortened" the family name for the sign on his storefront. Within the extended Scho(e)ttelkotte family, there are three Als married to Virginias, causing untold fun and confusion.

Yield: 6 servings

4 medium potatoes
1 small head cabbage, coarsely
  chopped

Salt to taste
Pinch sugar
8 to 10 bacon slices

Peel and quarter the potatoes and place them in a two-quart sauce pan. Add the cabbage, salt, sugar, and bacon. Add enough water to partially cover. Cook on a slow burner until well done, about one hour. Drain off all but two cups of the liquid. Remove the bacon and set aside; mash the mixture coarsely. Cube and brown the bacon. Add to the cabbage and potato mixture along with the drippings.

—Virginia Schoettelkotte
Rossmoyne

101

Polish Cabbage Rolls

(Go'Lumki)

Margaret's mother, who was from Poland, made this dish and served it with homemade dinner rolls.

Yield: 6 servings

1 medium head of cabbage	Pinch sage
1½ pounds ground beef (or half pork sausage, precooked to remove grease)	Salt to taste
	1 medium onion, chopped
	1 pound sauerkraut
1 cup cooked rice	1 29-ounce can tomatoes

Place the cabbage in a large pan or bowl. Pour boiling water over it to soften the leaves. While it is sitting in the water, mix the meat, rice, spices, and onion together. Cool the cabbage under cool water if necessary. Break off the leaves and place a portion of the meat mixture in each cabbage leaf. Roll it up like an envelope. Place in a small roasting pan. Pour the sauerkraut and tomatoes over the cabbage rolls and bake for one hour at 350 degrees F.

Note: This recipe can also be made successfully in a crockpot; set on low and let it cook all day.

—Margaret Mondron
Mt. Carmel

Cincinnati is a beautiful city; cheerful, thriving and animated. I have not often seen a place that commends itself so favourably and pleasantly to a stranger at the first glance as this does.

—*Charles Dickens, 1849*

Skyline of Cincinnati about 1841, from Kentucky shores. Drawing by Edward Timothy Hurley

Johnny Marzetti

Whether it's spelled Moussetti, Marziette, Mouzetti, Mousette, or Mousset, this dish is a basic guide for whipping up a quick casserole dinner from items you have on hand. Who is the infamous Johnny? No one seems to know, but he certainly got around.

Yield: 8 servings

2 cups chopped green pepper
1 cup chopped celery
2 cups chopped onion
1 pound ground beef
1 pound ground pork
¼ cup butter or margarine
2 teaspoons salt
½ cup stuffed olives, chopped
1 4-ounce can sliced mushrooms,
with liquid
1 10½-ounce can tomato soup
1 8-ounce can tomato sauce
1 8-ounce can tomato-mushroom
sauce
1 pound broad noodles
2 cups grated American cheese
(½ pound)

In a large skillet sauté the green pepper, celery, onion, and meats in hot butter. Add the salt, reduce the heat, and cook for about five minutes. Stir in the olives, mushrooms and liquid, soup, and sauces. Cook for another five minutes. Cook the noodles according to package directions, undercooking them slightly. Drain. Turn the noodles into a 14-by-10-inch roasting pan. Add the meat mixture. Stir gently until well mixed. Sprinkle the cheese on top. Bake for 35 minutes at 350 degrees F.

—Daisy E. Brosse
Mariemont

Rules for Serving

Cold food should be served on cold dishes; hot food on hot dishes.

When passing a dish, hold it so that the thumb will not rest upon the upper surface.

In passing dishes from which a person is to help himself, pass always to the left side, so that the food may be taken with the right hand.

In passing individual dishes, such as coffee, etc., set them down carefully from the right side.

Soiled dishes should be removed first, then food, then clean dishes, then crumbs.

Fill the glasses before every course, without lifting them from the table.

Never fill the glasses over three-fourths full.

Before dessert is served, remove the crumbs from the cloth with a brush, crumb knife or a napkin.

The hostess should serve the soup, salad, dessert, coffee, and at a family dinner, the vegetables and entrees.

The host serves the fish and meat.

Do not let the table become disorderly during the meal.

—Cincinnati Public Schools, 1900

Barbecued Ribs

When Eva throws a soul party, the menu includes two or three meats. But when she says "barbecue" she means ribs. Other items at her feast might include collard greens, corn pudding, sliced tomatoes, corn bread, and iced tea. For dessert what else but Sweet Potato Pie (see page 182) and good, hot coffee.

Whole sides of ribs, prepared by the
   butcher
Garlic powder to taste
Red pepper flakes to taste

Black pepper to taste
Cider vinegar as needed
Medium barbecue sauce as needed

Wash the ribs and season with the garlic powder, pepper flakes, and black pepper. Set aside for 30 minutes. Place the ribs over glowing coals and baste with vinegar while they are cooking, turning frequently, about 1½ hours. When the meat is cooked through, mop thoroughly with barbecue sauce and leave on the coals for an additional ten minutes, turning two or three times.

—Eva W. Henry
Maketewah

Sauerkraut 'n' Spareribs

Everybody in Cincinnati knows about sauerkraut. But what few people know about spareribs is that during the 1800s meat packing houses *gave away* the nearly bare rib bones for which we now pay premium prices! Could this fact have possibly influenced our culture?

Sauerkraut is usually cooked with pork to season, such as pork sausages or pig's knuckles, but by far the most common is the side of ribs. Simmered, covered, for at least an hour, the ribs can be left whole or broken and cut by the butcher into smaller pieces. The sauerkraut can be added at the beginning of the cooking or after 45 minutes or so when the grease and scum have been ladled off the broth. Accompanying the dish may be mashed potatoes, potato pancakes, noodles, dumplings, späetzles, dark rye bread, or biscuits.

Skillet Sauerkraut

Heat up some bacon fat in an iron skillet. Put in the sauerkraut and stir occasionally until heated through and lightly browned. You can put a lid on and steam at a real low temperature. Ham grease flavors well, but any will do.

—The Harry Pitzer family

Sweet and Sour Spareribs

Yield: 4 servings

1½ pounds spareribs (or one side of spareribs)
2 onions
2 green peppers
½ cup mixed Chinese pickle
1½ teaspoons sugar
1 tablespoon soy sauce

Salt and pepper to taste
1 cup pineapple, chopped
1 tablespoon lemon juice
2 teaspoons cornstarch
2 tablespoons water or pineapple juice

Have the butcher break or saw the spareribs in half lengthwise. Then chop or cut the pieces into individual bones. Place into a pot, cover with water, and simmer for about fifteen minutes. Remove the meat, reserving the cooking liquid. Chop the onions and peppers into small pieces and fry with the ribs in a hot pan with oil. Add a little broth, the spareribs, pickles, sugar, soy sauce, pepper, and salt to taste. Mix well. Simmer for another fifteen minutes, then add the pineapple and lemon juice. Thicken by adding the cornstarch which has been mixed with about two tablespoons of water or pineapple juice and let simmer for a few more minutes. Serve hot with cooked rice.

—*The International Folk Festival Cookbook*, prepared in 1979 for the tenth anniversary of the festival

Roasting Ye Olde Boar's Head

Already an ancient tradition when presented at Queens College, Oxford in 1340, the Boar's Head and Yule Log Festival is probably the oldest continuing festival of the Christmas season. It was a holiday tradition in manor houses in England and was first presented in America in Hoosic, New York in 1888. The first Cincinnati rendition was on the 600th anniversary of the Queens College presentation in 1940 at Christ Church. Each year since the story has been told with music, ceremony, and dance. The following is the Boar's Head "recipe" which, it must be understood, is meant for show and not for eating.

Set forth with spear and scutcheon to meat packing plant. Buy a fine, great "Head of Boar" which they will drably call "one head-pig.," no imagination! Bear same home right merrily, wrap ears and snout in ye olde aluminum foil, place whole in open roasting pan. Pry open mouth and wedge open with block of wood. Roast in 350 degree oven until brown enough to please you. Doesn't take too long, about 1½ to 2 hours. If a deeper shade of brown is desired, baste with milk and put back in oven for a few minutes. Helpful hints: while head is still warm, take out the block of wood and put in small red apple. Eyes may be decorated with cherries or cream cheese with cherries or with anything you would like to try. Boar's head is firmly anchored to a trencher, all of which is gaily decorated with holly, greens, mistletoe and fruits. The ears and the back of the great boar will need much decorating. If you sing "Caput apri defero" while it cooks, it will have extra flavor. Basting the cook in martinis gives extra flavor too, and enhances the whole procedure.

—Francis N. Mountel

107

Ham Baked in Rye Bread

This unusual recipe, brought over from Germany, was prepared by the Henry Luttmer Bakery on the east side of the city many years ago. For holidays, customers brought in their fifteen-pound precooked hams which the bakery covered with a thin layer of rolled out rye bread dough. It was then baked at a medium temperature for about two hours. The bread kept in the ham's juices, and although it didn't look appetizing when done, the crispy browned rye bread was edible. Luttmer's was housed in one side of a red brick building typical of the city's architecture. The storefront on the other side was a television shop with a bookie in the back room; thus is didn't take much coaxing to set a husband on an errand. Luttmer's moved in the fifties, changing the name to suit its new locale to the Mt. Washington Bakery.

Cottage Ham and String Beans

This most popular one-pot meal was known by old-timers as *gemuse*, pronounced "g'mersa" in German and meaning "vegetable," according to Karen Haldeman whose grandmother Lillian Niemiller-Meister was chief cook at Central Vocational High School for many years. The unwritten formula called for a cottage butt, a meaty hambone, or a couple of ham hocks; the vegetable, which could be string beans, kale, cabbage, or mixed greens; and red or new potatoes, carrots, rutabagas, turnips, or parsnips. The meat is simmered until tender and the vegetables added toward the end of the cooking, although in days gone by both meat and vegetables were simmered all day long. Karen and her husband David own butcher stand No. 8 at Findlay Market.

Country Ham Loaf

Yield: 10 to 12 servings

2 pounds ground ham
1 pound lean ground pork
2 eggs
20 small whole wheat crackers,
    rolled fine
2 tablespoons parsley

4 tablespoons chopped onion
2 tablespoons horseradish sauce
1 teaspon dry mustard
1 cup sour cream
Salt and pepper to taste

Apple Jelly Sauce

1 10-ounce jar apple jelly

1 tablespoon prepared mustard

Preheat the oven to 350 degrees F. Mix the ham, pork, eggs, and crackers. Then add all of the other ingredients and mix well. Form into a loaf and place in a roaster. Sprinkle lightly with flour and bake for 1½ hours.

Combine apple jelly with mustard, heat, and serve with ham loaf.

Note: For individual ham loaves, make into rounds about 3 or 4 inches in diameter and ¾-inch thick. Place a slice of pineapple on top of ham circle and make another ham circle with a hole in the middle like a doughnut. Bake as for regular ham loaf, only baking time will be less, about one hour. Baste with pineapple juice and serve with parsley placed in the hole.

—*Log House Cookbook,* 1981
Anderson Township Historical Society

Porkburgers

Pork, in every conceivable form, has had its influence on Cincinnati, once known as Porkopolis. It was the hog capital of the world, and as the bustling river town became "civilized," laws had to be passed against keeping pigs as pets and walking them down city sidewalks.

Yield: 8 servings

2 pounds ground pork
½ cup flour
½ teaspoon salt
¼ teaspoon white pepper
½ teaspoon dry mustard

2 tablespoons bacon fat
½ cup prune juice
½ cup port wine
¼ teaspoon caraway seeds

Shape the meat into patties. Roll the patties in the flour seasoned with the salt, pepper, and dry mustard. Brown on both sides in the bacon fat. Add the prune juice, wine, and seeds. Cover the pan and simmer for 45 minutes, stirring occasionally. Add water if necessary. Serve with noodles.
—Mrs. William Hauser
North Avondale

Grandpa's Wurst

This recipe has been in the Schwergaut family for generations. Although his sons and son-in-law help, father Bob is the master wurst maker, as his father and grandfather were before him. The sausage used to be smoked in a backyard smokehouse and processed in an old sausage press, but the recipe has been simplified to utilize a food grinder with a sausage attachment. Wurst making is a special event, the highlight being tasting time when thin patties are fried for sandwiches. It usually takes two or three samples before pronouncing the wurst suitable for putting into casings.

Yield: 15 to 20 patties or links

Garlic Water

6 garlic toes   1½ cups water

Wurst

2 tablespoons paprika   2 dashes allspice
2 teaspoons chili powder   Animal casings (optional)
2 tablespoons salt   5 pounds ground pork
1 teaspoon pepper

Wurst Making

To make the garlic water, crush the toes of garlic into the water and let stand six to eight hours or overnight.

To make the wurst mix together all of the seasonings. Place the pork in a large bowl or pot and poke thumb-size holes into the meat. Sprinkle the seasonings over the meat. Pour garlic water into the holes. Mix well with the hands, adding more garlic water as needed, using all of the water. Make into patties or put into animal casings.

110

Sloppy Beans and Cornbread

Thanks to the U.S. Senate, almost everyone in this country has a recipe for bean soup, but this recipe offers something different. In the Maxwell home in Oakley, Pete makes the beans and his wife Mary Catherine makes the cornbread.

Yield: 2 to 4 servings

Sloppy Beans

1 pound dry lima beans
½ pound pork, ham, or sausage
Cayenne pepper pod
1 large onion, chopped
1 potato, chopped (optional)
Salt and pepper to taste

Cornbread

2 strips bacon
1 cup cornmeal
1 cup white or whole wheat flour
1 cup sour milk or buttermilk
1 tablespoon sugar
2 teaspoons baking powder
½ teaspoon baking soda
½ teaspoon salt
3 tablespoons fat, oil, or melted butter
1 egg

Soak the beans overnight in cold water. Put them on to cook the next day, adding the meat and pepper pod. Simmer 2 to 3 hours. When the beans are getting soft, add the onion, potatoes, salt, and pepper. The

111

Albee Theatre—December 24, 1927 to September 17, 1974. This elegant movie house offered more than just movies. The house itself was always a part of the show, plus there were vaudeville-style performers and big bands, not to mention a twenty-two-piece house orchestra called the Albee Entertainers. The superb architecture and design of this grand masterpiece qualified it for inclusion on the National Register of Historic Places. "Get Your Man," with the "it" girl, Clara Bow, was the featured film on opening night and the price of admission was 35 cents. Drawing by Geneva South

112

vegetables should only cook the last half an hour or so. At the time you add the vegetables, make the cornbread.

Fry the bacon in a 10-inch iron skillet. Preheat the oven to 400 degrees F. Remove the bacon and crumble. Pour off all but about two tablespoons of the bacon grease, using in the cornbread for fat if desired. Keep the skillet hot. In a small bowl mix together the remaining cornbread ingredients and beat until well blended. Stir in the bacon bits. Pour the batter into the hot skillet and place it in the oven for about 20 minutes. It is done when set, and there will probably be a crack down the center. Serve the Sloppy Beans in a bowl, with the Cornbread and plenty of butter on the side.

Lagana

(A Greek "pizza")

About twenty years ago George Kalomeres remembered this dish his mother made when he was a child and persuaded her to prepare it once again. Since then it has become a family treat, served as a snack at parties and family events. The recipe was passed down to George's sister, Tasha Kalomeres Hill.

Yield: 2 pizzas

Dough

2 packages yeast	1 teaspoon salt
1 tablespoon sugar	7 cups white flour, divided
2 cups warm water, divided	¼ cup corn oil

Filling

½ pound bacon slices	½ pound feta cheese, crumbled
2 onions, chopped	2 tablespoons sesame seed
1 20-ounce carton cottage cheese, small curd	2 tablespoons parsley

Mix the yeast, sugar, and ½ cup warm water. Cover and allow to set in a warm place for 15 to 20 minutes. Add 1½ cups more warm water, salt, and 6 cups flour. Mix thoroughly. Then knead the dough, alternately adding the oil and remaining flour, kneading thoroughly after each addition. Set aside to rise to double the original volume. The dough will have an elastic texture but will not stick to the hands.

113

To make the filling, partially cook the bacon and remove from the skillet to drain. Pour off all but about 2 tablespoons of the bacon fat. Sauté the onions in the fat over a low heat. Place the cheeses in a bowl and mix in the sautéed onions, sesame seed, and parsley. When the dough has doubled, knead again and divide into two equal parts. Grease two pizza pans, and your hands, and press the dough into the pans. Add the cottage cheese mixture, spreading evenly over the top of both pans of dough. Place the bacon slices on top. Bake at 350 degrees F. for 40 to 45 minutes or until golden brown on the edges and top.

—Margeory Kalomeres

Skyline of Cincinnati in the 1880s, including the grand Suspension Bridge. Built in 1867, it is the oldest bridge across the Ohio River. It was closed by rising waters during the flood of 1884, but during the flood of 1937 it remained open and was Cincinnati's only link to Kentucky. Drawing by Timothy Edward Hurley

Mecklenburg Gardens Veal Americana

In 1865 Louis Mecklenburg opened a "bier gartens" similar to those in his native Germany. Wholesome food and drink were provided, and entertainment, generally initiated by the patrons, often took the form of a hearty "saengerfest." In the 1880s Mecklenburg's became a sort of civic center. To teach German immigrants to vote, mock elections were held for the mythical town of "Kloppenburg," the nickname for the neighborhood. In those days of twenty-one beers for a dollar, the male voters enjoyed refreshments while listening to campaigns for such offices as "Burgermeister" and "Schnutenkratzer" (Snoutscratcher). One could vote for the candidates of three parties—the Turkeys, the Sucklingpigs, and the Hares (replaced by the Suffragets in 1910). During prohibition faithful customers watched for a certain position of a toy ship on the back bar, a signal that libations stronger than near-beer were available in the speakeasy upstairs.

In recent years the distinguished restaurant earned a four-star rating serving an eclectic nouvelle French cuisine. However, the historic oak-beamed facility was located in a neighborhood plagued with crime and that, coupled with the economic recession of the day resulted in the decision to close on New Year's Eve 1982. Mecklenburg's will be sorely missed, but never forgotten.

Yield: 4 servings

Demi-Glaze

2 cups rich brown sauce
2 cups brown stock

¼ cup California cabernet
Salt and pepper to taste

Cutlets

4 5-ounce provimi veal cutlets
Salt and pepper to taste
1 cup butter
Juice of 1 lemon
¼ cup California cabernet
2 cups demi-glaze

4 ounces Smithfield or Kentucky
   ham, cut in 3-by-¼-inch strips
4 ounces Monterey Jack, cut in
   3-by-¼-inch strips
Lemon wedges for garnish
Parsley for garnish

To prepare the demi-glaze, combine the sauce with the stock and cook over a high heat until reduced to about 2 cups. Add the wine and heat through, about 3 minutes. Season to taste with the salt and pepper and

115

strain through a cheesecloth or fine sieve.

Pound the veal cutlets to about half of the original thickness to tenderize. Season with salt and pepper. Lightly flour each side. Heat the butter in a skillet until lightly browned, then add the veal cutlets and sauté about 40 seconds. Add the juice of 1 lemon. Turn the cutlets and pour on the cabernet. Sauté about 40 seconds. Place the cutlets on serving plates. Pour the demi-glaze into the skillet. Cook over high heat, uncovered, until reduced to about 1½ cups. Meanwhile crisscross the ham and cheese strips on top of each cutlet in a trellis pattern. Place under the broiler to melt cheese. Pour the glaze over cutlets. Garnish with lemon wedges and parsley. Serve with steamed asparagus and carrots.

Wiener Schnitzel

(Austrian)

In 1894 a group of six women got together and formed the Woman's City Club of Cincinnati in order to take on more civic responsibility. The club is still in existence, with a membership of over six hundred. In 1952 they published a book simply titled *Recipes*, a superior collection of locally representative foods.

Yield: 4 servings

4 veal chops or cutlets	½ pound fresh sardellin, soaked and
5 eggs	boned
2 tablespoons milk	½ pint sour cream
Salt and pepper to taste	1 tablespoon flour
Cracker crumbs, for coating	Juice of half lemon
Bacon fat for frying	Fresh parsley

Remove the bone from the chop if desired. Mix together one egg, milk, salt, and pepper. Dip the chops into the egg mixture, then into the cracker crumbs. Brown in hot fat on both sides. Set aside and keep warm. Remove all of the fat in the skillet except one tablespoon. Chop half of the sardellin finely and set aside. Mix the sour cream and flour and add to the skillet. Put in the chopped fish, add the lemon juice, and cook until thickened. Poach the remaining four eggs. To serve, remove the chops to a hot platter and cover each chop with a poached egg. Cut the remaining fish into long strips and place over the eggs. Pour the gravy around the platter and decorate with parsley.

Note: Sardellin, sardels or sardines are defined as any "small fish of the herring family." They are not as readily fresh here as they are in Europe. Sardines, canned in oil, may be used. Rinse them well, bone, and take off the skin.

—Mrs. Albert Kahn

Baked Catfish

Through the years Therese Hart's husband Tom fished in the Ohio River, the East Fork River, and in Kentucky rivers and lakes as many Cincinnatians still do, bringing home a croppie occasionally but most often catfish. To enjoy them as fresh as possible, the Harts kept the live fish in the bathtub half full with water. Their nieces and nephews, over for supper, would cautiously visit the doomed creatures, attempting to touch them without getting "finned." Tom wouldn't kill the fish, he left that job to Therese who stuck an ice-pick into the fish's head to kill it instantly. She would then scale the fish and clean out the insides. Although fried catfish was a favorite, an even more popular dish was the following recipe, which can easily be multiplied.

1 2-pound catfish, whole	Pinch sage, thyme, and parsley
1 small onion, chopped	Salt and pepper to taste
1 stalk celery, chopped	1 tablespoon salad oil
¼ cup butter	1 29-ounce can tomato sauce
1½ cups breadcrumbs	Juice of half a lemon

Scale and clean the fish and set aside. Sauté the onion and celery in the butter, then turn off the heat and add the breadcrumbs, sage, thyme, parsley, salt, and pepper to taste. Stir well, adding a little hot water if you prefer a moist dressing. Stuff the fish, and then rub it with the oil on both sides. Place it in a casserole dish and cover it with the tomato sauce. Squirt the lemon juice on top. Bake 30 to 45 minutes at 350 degrees F. or until the fish flakes when lifted with a fork. Serve with fresh asparagus.

—Therese Hart (Aunt Dee-dee)
Mt. Washington

Kedgerie

"Recipes which have stood the test of time and experience are of real worth. Those given in this cookbook have their roots in earlier days, and also live in the present. Many of them are coupled with happy memories of those who stood for the old traditions of excellent cooking and hospitality in Cincinnati."

Yield: 4 servings

1 cup rice	6 whole peppercorns
4 eggs, hard-cooked	1 bay leaf
2 pounds halibut	3 carrots, chopped

Curry Sauce

4 tablespoons butter	4 tablespoons flour
1 tablespoon chopped onion	Curry powder to taste

Boil the rice twenty minutes in a large quantity of water. Place in a colander and pour cold water over. Allow to drain. Place in a double boiler and allow it to steam until flaky, stirring frequently. Chop fine the eggs. Place the halibut in a pan with the peppercorns, bay leaf, and carrots; cover with water and poach until tender. Reserve the fish stock. Pick the fish apart into tiny pieces. To make the sauce, melt the butter in a small pan and add the onion. Sauté until slightly browned. Add the flour, stir until smooth, and let bubble on a low heat for two minutes. Add two cups of the fish stock and curry to taste, and simmer until thickened. Stir in the fish pieces. Serve over rice with hard-cooked egg pieces and Major Gray's Chutney on the side.

—Mrs. Alice Longworth
Garden Club of Cincinnati Cookbook, 1937

Anderson Ferry. This site was an Indian crossing long before Cincinnati or Constance, Kentucky were in existence. Since 1817 ferryboats have paddled back and forth for rush hour traffic. The popular ferry is also used by Cincinnatians as a shortcut to Latonia Race Track, or as part of a scenic route to Greater Cincinnati Airport, both in Kentucky. Drawing by Caroline Williams

Doris Day's Poached Salmon

Cincinnati's very respected and very own daughter Doris Day, took time from her family, her career pursuits, and her Pet Foundation (Box 600, Beverly Hills, CA 90213) to send us this recipe. With it comes an apology of sorts. "Unfortunately, I'm not much of a cook, but nevertheless I will give you one of my favorite recipes and I must tell you that I would rather eat it than try to cook it myself."

This is a recipe for poached salmon (either steaks or fillets, depending on whether or not you want to be bothered with bones). Use an iron pan and lay the fish flat on the bottom. Squeeze lemon over the fish and then pour enough vermouth or white wine over it to just cover the bottom of the pan. Add a little butter and sprinkle dill and parsley over the fish. Cover the pan with foil and simmer on a low to medium temperature until the fish appears done and flakes easily when prodded with a fork. Don't let the liquid boil, just simmer until done. If you wish, you can put it under the broiler for a few minutes to brown the top when it's done. Serve with hollandaise sauce.

119

Traditional Gefilte Fish

Yom Kippur, the day of atonement, is the last day of ten penitential days ushered in with the Jewish New Year, Rosh Hashana. Yom Kippur is observed by spending the entire period in total abstinence from food, drink, and work. It is the most solemn holy day of the Jewish calendar, starting at sundown on Yom Kippur Eve and ending the next evening when three stars appear in the sky and the ram's horn is blown at the conclusion of services. Many families break the fast with a light, non-meat meal. The Kramers start with a steaming bowl of lentil soup and challah (egg bread). Gefilte fish follows, with cheese blintzes, stewed fruits, and pastries. This *break-fast* with family, friends, and guests engenders hope for health, happiness, and friendship in the year to come.

Yield: about 3 dozen large pieces, or 100 small appetizers

Fish Stock

3 pounds whitefish	4 large onions, sliced
3 pounds buffalo fish	3 tablespoons salt
2 pounds yellow salmon	2 tablespoons white pepper
2 pounds mullet	3 tablespoons sugar

Fish Balls

4 large onions	3 tablespoons salt
1 cup matzoh meal	2 tablespoons white pepper
10 jumbo eggs (not extra large, jumbo)	3 tablespoons sugar
	4 large carrots, scraped clean

Bone and skin the fish, reserving bones, skin, and meat.

To make the stock, make a nest of the bones at the bottom of the pot. Add the onions. Half fill the pot with water and add the salt, pepper, and sugar. Bring to a boil. While waiting, be sure all the bones have been removed from the fish. Rinse skin thoroughly and set aside.

To make the fish balls, put the boned fish through a grinder twice, using a rough blade. Put the onions through, using a fine blade. Work the onions through the fish using a hand chopper. Add the meal and blend with the hand chopper until you have a fluffy mixture. Add the eggs, salt, pepper, and sugar, and blend again.

When the fish stock has come to a boil, prepare the fish balls. Have a dish of water nearby to moisten hands so fish does not stick to your hands. Form balls the size of a medium egg and flatten slightly. Drop into the boiling stock, side by side. Shake the pot occasionally to make sure the nest is not sticking. As the pot fills, extra water may have to be added to keep the balls covered, but use as little as possible. When all the balls are in the pot, reduce the heat to medium. Cover the fish balls with the fish skin and add the whole carrots. Cook for 2½ hours, shaking the pot vigorously during the cooking to make sure the bones and onions do not stick. The liquid should evaporate during the cooking by roughly one-fourth.

Cool throughly; the fish balls will fall apart if removed from warm stock. Set carrots aside. Put the fish in china, plastic, or glass containers since fish picks up a metal taste. Strain the stock and pour over fish not more than one inch deep. Freeze the remaining stock. Refrigerate the fish and carrots for at least three days. At serving time put the fish plus gel on platters and place a carrot slice on each. Serve with freshly ground horseradish. (See page 207.)

—Fradie Kramer
North Avondale

Scampi alla La Rosa

The LaRosa name is synonymous with delicious and economical Italian food in Cincinnati. A family enterprise, there are thirty-six pizzerias in the area plus a grocery, wine store, and the original warm and friendly Italian Inn Restaurant on Boudinot Avenue.

Yield: 1 to 2 servings

5 ounces butter	6 medium mushrooms, sliced
2 garlic cloves	Salt and pepper to taste
12 large shrimp, peeled and deveined	Juice from ½ medium lemon
	4 ounces dry white wine
2 cups white flour	8 sprigs parsley, chopped fine

Melt the butter in a large skillet over medium heat. Add the garlic and sauté until brown but not burned. Remove, chop finely, and set aside. Toss the shrimp in the flour, place in the skillet, add the mushrooms, and sauté until golden brown. Season with salt and pepper. Top with the lemon and wine, and let simmer for 2 or 3 minutes. To serve, sprinkle with the chopped garlic and parsley.

—Mark LaRosa

121

Fettucini Ginocchio

The Ginocchio family dates back to the 1840s in Cincinnati, and this is a very old Italian recipe. Green and white pasta is used although Louie recommends using red pasta also, when available, made from tomato, pimento, flour, and egg.

Yield: 4 servings

1 pound fettucini
1 garlic clove, crushed
1 tablespoon rosemary
2 tomatoes, peeled, seeded, and
   chopped
2 dashes Maggi

½ cup (1 stick) butter
1 pound medium-large shrimp,
   slightly cooked
1 teaspoon basil
Parmesan cheese

Boil the pasta in salted water until firm, al dente (to the teeth). While the pasta is boiling, sauté the garlic, rosemary, tomatoes, and Maggi in the butter over a very low heat until the tomatoes are soft. Add the shrimp and stir well. Drain and rinse the pasta, and then toss it with the basil. Place the pasta on a platter, cover with the shrimp sauce, and sprinkle with Parmesan cheese to serve.

—Louis Ginocchio
Watch Hill

Asparagus Mousse with Seafood Rice Salad

Because of her vast repertoire of international recipes, Lauretta was proclaimed one of the "Best Cooks in Town" by *The Cincinnati Post.* She served this delectable entrée at a luncheon for League of Women Voters board members during the summer of 1981. The entire menu included seasonal fruits, crusty sesame bread sticks, French minted tea, chocolate, and butterscotch brownies. The tea and butterscotch brownies are included in this book.

Yield: 6 to 8 servings

Mousse

1 envelope unflavored gelatin
¼ cup cold water
2 10-ounce cans of asparagus;
   drain, reserving liquid, and mash
1½ cups small curd cottage cheese

½ cup chopped almonds
¼ cup mayonnaise
2 teaspoons lemon juice
1 teaspoon salt
1 teaspoon Dijon-type mustard

122

Seafood Rice Salad

1 cup cooked shrimp pieces
1 cup cooked crab pieces
1 cup cooked rice
1 carrot, grated
15 to 20 sliced black olives
¼ cup chopped pimento

3 tablespoons mayonnaise
  (homemade preferred)
Juice of half a lemon
1 10-ounce can asparagus, drained
  and cut up

Soften the gelatin in the water. Bring to a boil the asparagus liquid; add the softened gelatin. Remove from the heat and stir until it is dissolved. Chill until slightly thickened. Combine the remaining mousse ingredients with the thickened gelatin. Pour into a lightly oiled 4 to 5 cup ring mold and chill 24 hours.

To make the salad, toss all of the ingredients except the asparagus together in a chilled bowl. Add the asparagus and toss again lightly. Just before serving unmold the mousse, fill with the seafood and rice salad, and serve. Put any extra salad in a side dish.

—Lauretta Omeltschenko
Western Hills

Le Coquilles St. Jacques et Homard aux Fine Herbes

The Maisonette—priceless jewel in the Queen City's crown—shares this recipe served during the "Taste of America" inaugural festivities in Washington, D.C., 1981. The Comisars, who also own three other local restaurants, have earned their aristocratic position in the world of fine cuisine.

Yield: 4 servings

2 pounds fresh lobster
Fish stock as needed
1 pound fresh baby scallops
  (Chatham)
Salt and pepper to taste

½ pint heavy cream
1 tablespoon chopped fresh parsley
1 tablespoon chopped fresh chives
  or green onion
1 teaspoon chopped fresh tarragon

Cook the lobster in a strong fish stock. Cut and remove all of the meat and chop it ½-inch thick. Keep it warm. Reduce the stock to half its volume and strain. Put the scallops in a heavy skillet, cover them barely with the hot fish stock, and add salt and pepper. Bring to a boil, remove the scallops, and keep them warm. Add the cream to the skillet and reduce it until the sauce coats the spoon. Add the scallops and the lobster to the sauce. Add the fine herbs; do not boil any more. Serve immediately.

Note: You can use the lobster tail shell as a garnish around the plate.

Side Dishes

Italian Asparagus

This recipe, one of several given by Carmela to Visitation Church's *The Dinner Bell* cookbook, came from her mother who was from Campobasso, Italy.

2 pounds fresh asparagus
1 cup (2 sticks) butter or margarine
¼ teaspoon pepper

1 tablespoon grated Romano
   cheese
4 slices Mozzarella cheese

Steam the asparagus almost tender. Preheat oven to 325 degreees F. Melt the butter slowly in a pan; add pepper and Romano and mix well. Place the drained asparagus in a pie plate and pour melted butter over the vegetables. Bake for about 10 minutes, then add 4 or more slices of Mozzarella. Return to the oven until melted.

Note: Broccoli may be fixed in exactly the same manner.

—Carmela Orlando
Western Hills

Mother's Baked Beans

Yield: 12 servings

2 pounds navy, great northern, or
   marrow fat beans
1 10-ounce bottle ketchip
1 cup brown sugar
2 teaspoons dry mustard
½ cup molasses

1 tablespoon Worcestershire sauce
Salt and pepper to taste
1 pound salt pork or bean bacon,
   sliced
1 large onion

Wash the beans and pick over carefully. Cover with three inches of water in a large pot and soak overnight. In the morning, drain and cover well with fresh water. Bring to a boil and simmer until several beans held in a spoon and blown upon burst their skin (about two hours or more). Drain beans, reserving the cooking water. Put the ketchup, brown sugar, mustard, molasses, Worcestershire sauce, salt, and pepper into the beans and mix well. Taste and adjust the flavoring if necessary. Place half of the salt pork or bacon in the bottom of a large bean pot. Pour bean mixture over the meat. Press onion, whole, down into the center of the beans. Take the remaining half of the meat and press into the beans rind side up. Add some bean water, making beans liquid. Bake at 250 degrees F. for 6 to 8 hours. Anytime beans look too dry, add a little more liquid. The beans will be done when they are tender but separate, not soft and mashed looking.

—Marjorie A. Frame

Liver Dumplin's

Lois Clark is a collector of cookbooks. This old recipe is her mother's, and she has never seen one like it in any cookbook. It is easy and delicious and the dumplings can be served hot or cold.

Yield: 4 servings

1 pound fresh liver
½ pound bacon
1 large onion
1 teaspoon nutmeg

1 teaspoon salt
½ teaspoon pepper
6 to 8 tablespoons white flour

Grind the liver, bacon, and onion together in a food grinder. Add the seasonings and enough flour to make a soft doughy mixture the consistency of a dumpling batter. Drop by the tablespoon into boiling water, bring back to a boil, and then reduce the heat to medium. Cover and cook for 15 minutes.

—Lois E. Clark

Stewed Tomatoes

This was a favorite lunchroom dish with children attending St. Rose School on Eastern Avenue during the 1940s and 1950s when Rose was Chief Cook.

Yield: 6 to 8 servings

1 2-pound can tomatoes
Sugar, salt, and pepper to taste

1 or 2 slices day-old bread
1 tablespoon butter

Cut the tomatoes in small pieces. Bring the tomatoes, sugar, salt, and pepper to a boil. Reduce the heat and simmer about 10 minutes. Remove from heat. Cut the bread into 1-inch squares. Add the butter and bread to the tomatoes, blending lightly.

—Rose Litkenhaus
Columbia-Tusculum Historical District

127

Pineapple Beets

Yield: 6 to 8 servings

2 tablespoons cornstarch
1 cup pineapple juice, divided
½ cup sugar
¼ cup cider vinegar
1 teaspoon lemon juice

1 tablespoon butter or margarine
1 pound fresh beets, sliced and
   cooked or 1 1-pound can, drained
½ cup crushed pineapple

In the top of a double boiler, combine the cornstarch and pineapple juice; stir to make a smooth paste. Add the remaining pineapple juice, sugar, vinegar, and lemon juice and stir again. Cook over a low heat until clear and thick, about 8 minutes, stirring frequently. Add the butter, crushed pineapple, and drained beet slices. Stir. Serve hot, garnished with summer savory if desired.

—Mary Jean Stoutemyer
A Book of Favorite Recipes, 1981

Findlay Market

Findlay Market, the first suburb to be annexed to Cincinnati, was named after General James Findlay who owned the property. Findlay was a proprietor of a prosperous log cabin store which was founded in 1793. He eventually became mayor of Cincinnati.

Originally the area was simply designated an open air market for farmers, but in 1852 a cornerstone was laid for an open-sided, cast iron market building which would cost $12,000. It was an immense success.

In 1902 the market house was enclosed and refrigeration was added. With its colorful vegetable, fruit, and flower stands along the curbs, and stores of every description around the square, Findlay Market became Cincinnati's first shopping center, reflecting its German heritage later intermingled with the Italian.

Inside, patrons may purchase every conceivable cut of meat plus fish from lakes, rivers, streams, and from the faraway oceans. Imported cheeses and sausages are available, along with spices from all over the world, bakery goods, candies, fresh chickens, eggs, and tub butter from local farms. Outside, the kiosks display products from the garden, field, orchard, and vineyard tempting to the eye as well as to the tastebuds. And the cheerful noises all around, as merchants vie for customers, create a joyful atmosphere like that of centuries ago.

Always changing, yet always the same, there is only one quaint, historic, wonder-full Findlay Market.

Findlay Market.....1969

The Race Street end of Cincinnati's celebrated Findlay Market in historic Over-The-Rhine. Drawing by Geneva South

Carrots and Grapes

Yield: 6 servings

3 cups fresh carrots, sliced
1/4 cup butter
2 teaspoons cornstarch
1/4 teaspoon salt

1 teaspoon lemon juice
1/3 cup honey
1/8 teaspoon cinnamon
1 cup green grapes, halved

Cook the carrots in a small amount of water until they are tender. Drain them well and set aside. In a small pan, melt the butter and blend in the cornstarch until smooth. Add the salt, lemon juice, honey, and cinnamon. Boil three minutes or until thick and clear. Add the carrots to the sauce, heating gently. Just before serving add the grapes.

—Joan Simons, *Rivertown Recipes*, 1980

Potato Dumplings

(Kartoffel Klosse)

This classic appeared in a cookbook titled *Two-Hundred and Thirty-Four Extra Special Recipes*, compiled by the Junior Members of the Ohio Library Association, Cincinnati Public Library, in 1951. Some people claim the mashed potatoes should be refrigerated overnight for best results.

Yield: 12 dumplings

2 cups mashed potatoes (leftovers
    are okay)
1 tablespoon butter
1 tablespoon onion, chopped fine
1 egg
3/4 cup flour

1 1/2 teaspoons salt
1/8 teaspoon pepper
1 cup 1/4-inch bread cubes fried in
    butter
Buttered breadcrumbs for garnish

Heat mashed potatoes, add butter, and then cool. Add onion and egg; mix thoroughly with a fork. Sift in the flour, salt, and pepper and blend well. Shape into twelve balls the size of an egg, forming each around 4 or 5 cubes of bread. Cook gently in boiling water for seven minutes. Serve with sauerbraten or other meat dish, on a large platter. Sprinkle dumplings with breadcrumbs which have been browned in a frying pan with a small amount of butter.

—Rita Bechtold
Cincinnati Public Library Catalog Department

130

Gnocchi alla Romano

This delectable preparation is a tasteful accompaniment to standing rib roast, lamb, or fowl.

Yield: 6 to 8 servings

5 cups milk
½ cup (1 stick) butter, divided
1 scant teaspoon salt
Sprinkling white pepper
Dash nutmeg

1½ cups semolina
2 egg yolks mixed with
  2 tablespoons milk
1¾ cups grated Parmesan or
  Pecorino cheese

Place the milk, six tablespoons of the butter, salt, pepper, and nutmeg in the top of a double boiler and heat over a low flame. In the meantime, place water in the bottom of the double boiler and bring to a boil. Bring the milk mixture to a gentle boil, and then add the semolina in a slow stream, stirring vigorously with a wooden spoon to break up lumps. Beat until smooth and thick. Insert the pot into the bottom of the double boiler and continue cooking and stirring for 20 minutes or until the wheat cooks away from the side of the pot and the mixing spoon stands upright. Remove from heat and cool for about ten minutes. Add the egg yolks and milk, plus half of the cheese. Beat well. Pour the mixture into a buttered jellyroll pan, cookie sheet, or onto a marble slab; spread it out with a metal spatula dipped in hot water to a layer ½-inch thick. Refrigerate for several hours. If refrigerated overnight, cover with aluminum foil. Remove any wrapping carefully to avoid water condensation getting on the gnocchi. Preheat oven to 400 degrees F. Grease a shallow baking dish. Shape the gnocchi into rounds using a biscuit cutter dipped in water. Rebuild the scraps until all of the mixture is used. Melt the remaining butter. Line the rounds in the baking dish, slightly overlapping, and brush each generously with the melted butter. Sprinkle with the remaining cheese. Bake in the center of the oven for 20 minutes or until the rounds are golden and the edges slightly browned. Place under a broiler for one minute if you like a crisper, crustier surface. Serve hot with extra Parmesan on the side. Benvenuti signore et signori, buon appetito!

—Mary Valerio
Valerio's Restaurant

Summer Squash Casserole

Yield: 6 servings

7 cups sliced yellow squash
¼ cup chopped onion
1 12-ounce can cream of chicken
  soup

1 cup sour cream
1 cup shredded carrots
¼ cup butter, melted
3 cups herb stuffing mix

Cook the squash and onion in very little water until tender. Drain well. Preheat oven to 350 degrees F. Combine the soup, sour cream, and carrots in a large bowl. Fold in the vegetables. Toss the stuffing in butter. Spread half of the stuffing in a greased 7-by-12-inch pan. Spoon the vegetable mixture on top. Sprinkle the rest of the stuffing mix on top. Bake for 25 to 30 minutes or until heated through.

—Joan Simons
Rivertown Recipes, 1980

Grit Casserole

Cincinnati is known as the "northernmost southern city," and the South has had a tremendous influence on Cincinnati cooking. This casserole started out in Texas, found its way to Atlanta, and comfortably moved in next to the baked beans and potato salads at the annual Parchman and Oyler (now Coldwell Banker) Realtors picnic.

Yield: 6 to 8 servings

¾ cup quick grits
3 cups boiling water
⅓ pound sharp Cheddar cheese,
  grated
2 eggs, well-beaten

¾ stick butter, at room temperature
1 teaspoon salt
6 drops hot pepper sauce
Paprika for garnish

Cook the grits in the water, boiling until they are dry. Preheat oven to 350 degrees F. Combine the cheese, eggs, butter, salt, and hot pepper sauce in a bowl and blend into the hot grits. Pour into a greased 2-quart casserole dish and sprinkle the top with paprika. Bake for 1½ hours.

—Jane Mathys
Miamiville

Best Roasted Corn-on-the-Cob

This was a specialty Pete prepared for family eat-outs in the old Cincinnati Milling Machine (now Milacron) picnic grounds in Oakley.

Fresh corn-on-the-cob, unshucked   Butter, salt, and pepper to taste

Plunge the corn into a bucket of cold water and let it sit "while you play tennis"—a direct reference to the many popular tennis courts at the Mill. While the coals are heating, shuck the corn almost to the bottom of the cob and remove as much of the silk as possible. Rub with butter and sprinkle with salt and pepper. Pull the shucks back up and tie at the top with a piece of shuck or string. Place the corn on an outdoor grill and cover them with a wet, wrung-out gunny sack to keep in the steam. Roast 15 to 20 minutes, turning frequently, or until the corn is cooked through and smells irresistible.

—Pete Maxwell
Oakley

Millcreek Potatoes

It is likely this dish was originally named after an important waterway. Now, however, the word Millcreek is apt to bring forth thoughts of an expressway of the same name!

Cut the potatoes into pieces the size of a large raisin and set aside. Put into a skillet a sufficient quantity of milk to about cover the potatoes. Add a piece of butter the size of an egg, one teaspoon flour thinned with a little cold milk, salt and pepper to taste. When the milk boils add the potatoes and cook until the milk is nearly absorbed. Shake the skillet frequently to prevent burning, but do not stir the potatoes. Serve very hot.

—Practical Receipts of Experienced
Housekeepers *by the Ladies of the*
Seventh Presbyterian Church of
Cincinnati, 1878

Carrots O'Brien

Cook large carrots in boiling salted water until tender, then drain, cover with cold water, and slip the skins from them. Cut in matchlike pieces. Cut a green pepper, freed from its seeds, into long thin strips and do the same with one canned pimento. Fry carrots and green pepper in Crisco, taking care they do not brown. Add the pimento and cook a few moments longer. Season to taste, and sprinkle a teaspoon of lemon juice and one of finely chopped parsley over the dish before serving.

—New Recipes *pamphlet*
Procter & Gamble, 1930

Easy Potato Pancakes

Don't bother grating if you have a food processor or blender. Make these extra special spuds at the last minute or they will discolor.

Yield: 4 to 6 servings

3 eggs
1 small onion, quartered
3 tablespoons flour

Salt, pepper, and nutmeg to taste
3 potatoes, cut in pieces

Place all of the ingredients into the food processor for about half a minute, or place the ingredients into the blender in the order given, adding two tablespoons of water when you put in the eggs and adding the potato pieces a few at a time. Fry just like pancakes in a little oil on a griddle or in a skillet. Repeat the recipe for more pancakes. Serve alone or with sour cream and applesauce.

Note: The potatoes need not be peeled.

—Lite Papke

Cauliflower Casserole

Yield: 6 servings

1 medium head cauliflower, broken into flowerettes
1 cup grated Cheddar or American cheese, divided
1 small onion, chopped
2 tablespoons parsley
3 tablespoons butter

3 cups chopped fresh or 2½ cups canned tomatoes
1 beef bouillon cube
1 tablespoon sugar
Salt and pepper to taste
3 tablespoons breadcrumbs

Cook the cauliflower in salted water. Drain well or dry with a turkish towel. Place the flowerettes in a greased casserole dish and lightly toss with ¾ cup of the grated cheese. Preheat oven to 350 degrees F. Brown the onion and parsley in the butter. Add the tomatoes, bouillon cube, sugar, salt, pepper, and the breadcrumbs. Mix well, and then simmer for five minutes. Pour over the cauliflower. Sprinkle with the remaining cheese and bake until heated through, about 30 minutes.

Note: This tomato sauce can be used to make a zucchini casserole also; use white cheese instead of yellow, such as Monterey Jack or Mozzarella.

—Charlene Dittrich
Mack

Fine Cottage Cheese

Let the milk be turned by rennet, or by setting it in a warm place. It must not be heated, as the oily parts will then pass off, and the richness is lost. When fully turned, put it in a coarse linen bag, and hang it to drain several hours, till all the whey is out. Then mash it fine, salt it to the taste, and thin it with good cream, or add but a little cream and roll it into balls.

It also makes a fine pudding, by thinning it with milk, and adding eggs and sugar, and spice to the taste, and baking it. Many persons use milk when turned for a dessert, putting on sugar and spice. Children are fond of it.

—Miss Beecher's Domestic Receipt Book, 1868

Rutabaga in Sour Cream

Yield: 6 servings

4 cups peeled and cubed
   rutabaga
Salt and pepper to taste
1 medium onion, sliced

2 tablespoons butter
1 cup sour cream
½ teaspoon caraway or dill
   seeds

Cook the rutabaga in a small amount of boiling salted water for about 20 minutes or until tender. Drain well. Sprinkle with salt and pepper. Sauté the onion in butter until it is tender. Add to the sour cream. Pour over the cooked rutabaga. Sprinkle with caraway or dill seed.

—*The Log House Cookbook*, 1980
Anderson Township Historical Society

Noodle Casserole

Lately cooks shy away from these sinfully rich recipes, but this old Jewish delight ought to be tried at least once.

Yield: 8 servings

1 10-ounce package noodles
½ cup (1 stick) butter
½ pint sour cream

1 12-ounce carton cottage cheese
Salt to taste
2 eggs beaten

Boil the noodles according to package directions. Preheat the oven to 350 degrees F. and heat the butter in a baking dish until brown. Drain and combine the noodles with the sour cream, cottage cheese, salt, and eggs. While still warm place the noodle mixture into the buttered dish. Bake in the middle of the oven for 1 hour. Cut in squares to serve.

—Maey Schott and Florence Shulman
Western Hills

Fried Green Tomatoes

This is the ultimate Midwestern delicacy.

Firm green tomatoes
Salt and pepper to taste
Flour and cornmeal, half and half

Bacon grease for frying
Longhorn cheese (optional)

136

Cut the tomatoes into ½-inch slices. Roll or shake in the seasoned flours. Brown each side in the bacon grease. Place a small piece of cheese, smaller than the tomato, on tomato slices if desired. The tomatoes should be slightly soft on the inside, but firm and crisp on the outside when done. If the insides fall apart they have either been overcooked or the tomato was beginning to ripen.

Note: Some people dip the tomato slices in buttermilk before breading.

To serve green tomatoes for breakfast, make a milk gravy from the remaining flours and grease; serve with eggs, toast, and grits.

—Therese Hart (Aunt Dee-dee)
Mt. Washington

Sweet and Sour Red Cabbage

This familiar recipe includes the pressure cooker method, that "instant" potboiler so popular in the 1940s.

Yield: 6 servings

1 medium red cabbage, shredded	1 tablespoon flour
4 tablespoons fat, preferably chicken or beef	½ teaspoon allspice
	1 teaspoon salt
2 tablespoons sugar	5 tablespoons vinegar
1 tart apple, peeled and thinly sliced	2 cups boiling water

Cook all of the ingredients together twenty minutes, covered, stirring occasionally. (In a pressure cooker use one-half cup boiling water and cook at 15 pounds for eight minutes.)

—from *Manna a la Carte;*
Not all—Just Most of the Best Recipes
From Homes on the Seven Hills and
Gateway to the South, 1950

King's Island-International Street. The Royal Fountain, 320 feet long, 80 feet wide, with 106 water jets shooting 10,000 gallons into the air at one time, is the park's impressive first view. At night 336 lights of different colors provide guests with a thrilling and vibrant water kaleidoscope. At fountain's end stands the park's landmark—the Eiffel Tower, an actual one-third size replica of the original in Paris. Drawing by Paul Blackwell, courtesy of Row House Gallery, Milford

King's Island Fresh Cut French Fries

Coney Island is only a memory, as Parker's Grove was to our grandparents. But the children at heart today have King's Island, chosen by the American Coaster Enthusiasts to be the best amusement park in the country. These French fries are one of the park's favorite food features.

Idaho potatoes, very large (10 ounces each or better)   Cooking oil for frying

Wash the potatoes well but do not peel. Cut them with a ⅝-inch square cutter. Place in cold water so that they do not discolor. When you are ready to use them, dry them well. Blanch in the oil for 7 minutes at 250

138

degrees F. Remove and cool to room temperature for at least a half hour. Finish off in the oil for 2½ to 3 minutes more at 350 degrees F. Salt and serve with ketchup and malt vinegar.

—Bill Bell
Food Service Director,
King's Island

Späetzle

Yield: 16 to 24 servings

4 cups flour
8 eggs
4½ eggshells water (about ¼ cup)

½ cup (1 stick) butter, browned
1 cup buttered croutons

Place the flour in a large pottery bowl. Make a well in the center and add the eggs and water. Beat with a wooden spoon until the dough is elastic and not sticking to the sides. It takes awhile. (Note: Some people let the batter rest an hour at this point.) Press the batter through a späetzle press into four quarts of rapidly boiling, salted water. Do one press-full at a time, and then rinse. If you do not have a press, try pressing the batter through a wet colander with big holes. You can also place the batter into the boiling water for a few seconds, then remove to a cutting board and cut it off in thin strips with a sharp, wet knife into the boiling water. When the späetzles rise to the top of the water and cook over to one side, they are finished and can be removed with a slotted spoon to the colander. Place them in a heated bowl and pour the browned butter and croutons over them. Serve with sauerbraten gravy.

Note: Späetzels can be made the day before. To reheat, pour them back into a large pot of boiling water. Turn off heat immediately. Let stand two minutes and drain.

—Elsie Firstos
Westwood

Pot of Greens

Particularly favored by the Black community, greens are a delicious and nutritious asset to any menu. They can be cooked separately or together to blend their harmonious flavors. In Greek households, cultivated dandelion greens are cooked in a similar fashion and served with lemon wedges. Wild dandelions, mustards, and pokeweed make a perfectly suitable addition. If you happen on a bitter bunch, pour off the first boiling waters, add new water, and continue the cooking.

Yield: 6 to 8 servings

About 2 pounds mixed greens (mustard, collards, kale, or turnips)
1 large onion, chopped

2 ounces salt pork, chopped
2 strips seasoning bacon, chopped
1 cayenne pepper pod
Salt to taste

Wash the greens well in a basin of warm water, drain, and wash again. Place in a pot and add about a quart of water. Add all of the other ingredients, bring to a boil, and then simmer, uncovered, for about an hour. Add more water only if necessary; let the greens cook down. Greens can be eaten as a side dish or a whole meal with cornbread. Be sure to taste some of the cooking water, known as "Pot Liquor" in the South.

—Millie Jenkins
Over-the-Rhine Historical District

Puffballs and Morels

Cincinnatians are frugal cooks and nothing is more frugal than free ingredients such as mushrooms. Puffballs and morels are two of the easiest to hunt in these parts. Of course, all naturalists caution you to learn how to identify wild edibles before bringing them into the kitchen; many Cincinnatians qualify as experts.

Puffballs, the more common of the two, are round, smooth, and white, and should only be eaten when they are fresh and not turning yellow inside. They are usually about eight to fifteen inches in diameter, sometimes very large, and are attached to the ground by a sort of cord. They are solid all the way through. Puffballs are found in cultivated and waste lands and at the edges of woods and fields from August to October.

Puffballs may be sliced like a loaf of bread, breaded, seasoned, and fried like French toast.

The morel, sometimes called a "sponge" mushroom, has an oval or pyramid-shaped cap, and is deeply and widely pitted or pocked, with the ridges grayish, whitish or pale tan. The stem is whitish. Beware of confusing them with false morels which are more wrinkled—check pictures in books or nature museums. These popular mushrooms can be found from May to September in apple orchards and in maple or beech woods. These too must be eaten fresh, before any discoloration.

Both puffballs and morels are delicious sliced or chopped and added to gravies, particularly beef juices, or sautéed in butter. They can be used in place of cultivated mushrooms in most recipes and can also be added to salads.

—Vivian Wagner
Caldwell Nature Center

Baked Eggplant

Yield: 10 to 12 servings

2 medium eggplants
6 eggs
1¼ cups milk
Salt and pepper to taste

3½ cups cracker crumbs
3 cups grated Cheddar or American cheese
1½ cups butter or margarine, melted

Peel, chop, and boil the eggplants until tender. Drain in a colander for fifteen minutes. Pour into a bowl. Add the eggs, milk, seasonings, half of the cracker crumbs, half of the grated cheese, and half of the margarine. Mix well. Grease a 9-by-13-inch baking dish and pour in the eggplant mixture. Sprinkle the top with the remaining cheese, cracker crumbs, and margarine. Bake at 450 degrees F. until golden brown and firm, 30 to 40 minutes.

—Rose Thompson, Cook
Phillips Towboat
Ohio River Co.

Breads and Breakfasts

Heidelberg Rye Bread

The donor of this authentic recipe is a locally well-known international cook. Hailing from New York, she describes Cincinnati as a cosmopolitan town—very much like a "little New York."

Yield: 2 loaves

3 cups white flour
2 packages dry yeast
¼ cup cocoa
1 tablespoon sugar
1 tablespoon salt
1 tablespoon caraway seeds
2 tablespoons dehydrated onion

flakes (optional)
⅓ cup brown sugar
2 tablespoons butter or margarine, at room temperature
2 cups hot water
2½ to 3½ cups rye flour
Salad oil for gloss

Combine the white flour, yeast, cocoa, sugar, salt, and caraway seeds (plus onion flakes if desired) in a large bowl. Stir to blend. Mix in the brown sugar and butter. Add the hot water and beat with a mixer at high speed for one minute. With a wooden spoon gradually stir in just enough rye flour to make a soft dough which leaves the sides of the bowl. Turn onto a floured board. Knead five minutes. Dough will be slightly sticky. Cover with plastic wrap and set aside twenty minutes. Punch down. Divide dough in half. Shape each portion into a round loaf, 8 inches in diameter, and flatten slightly. Place into greased 8-inch pie pans or on a greased baking sheet. Brush the dough lightly with oil. Cover the pan loosely with plastic wrap and refrigerate 2 to 24 hours. When ready to bake remove from the refrigerator and uncover. Preheat oven to 400 degrees F. Let stand 10 minutes. Cut an X in the top of the loaves with a sharp knife. Bake for 30 to 40 minutes. Cover loosely with foil if the crust browns too quickly. Remove from pans immediately and cool on a rack.

Note: For party rye, brush the top with slightly beaten egg white and sprinkle on kosher salt.

—Rose Marie Gigliotti
Mt. Washington

Beer Bread

This simple formula doesn't turn up in old cookbooks, but some claim it is an old recipe. It was an extremely popular 1982 recipe in this brewery town.

Yield: 1 loaf

3 cups self-rising flour
2 tablespoons sugar

1 12-ounce bottle of beer

Mix all of the ingredients together. Place in a greased 9-by-5-inch loaf pan. Bake at 350 degrees F. for approximately 45 minutes. Brush with butter or margarine if desired.

Irish Barm Brack

This "speckled bread" is traditionally eaten at Halloween in Ireland. A ring is beaten in with the batter and according to legend, whoever the recipient is will be married within the year. It is reprinted from the popular Children's Hospital cookbook first published in 1966 and still in print today. The unique feature of the book, besides some excellent recipes, is the collection of original drawings by Cincinnati artist Caroline Williams.

Yield: 1 loaf

1 cup cold tea
1 cup brown sugar, packed
1 pound dried fruit (raisins, currants,
    candied peel, etc.)
2 cups whole wheat or white flour

or a mixture
2 teaspoons baking powder
1 beaten egg
1 ring (optional)

Place in a bowl and soak together overnight the tea, brown sugar, and dried fruit. The next morning add the flour, baking powder, and egg and mix thoroughly. Add the ring. Bake in a greased pan for approximately 1¼ hours at 325 degrees F. Remove from the tin when cooled somewhat. Slice thickly when warm or thinly when completely cooled. Serve well buttered.

Note: To prevent fruit from sinking to the bottom of the batter, remove it from the liquid after soaking and toss with a little flour. Add last to the batter.

—Mrs. William Powles
The Cincinnati Cook Book, 1966

145

Yeast Rolls

This was May's mother's handy recipe anytime the family had a hankerin' for homemade rolls.

Yield: 3½ to 4 dozen rolls

1 cup boiling water	1 cup cold water
⅓ cup sugar	2 eggs
¼ cup shortening	6 cups flour
1 cake or package yeast	1 tablespoon salt

Blend the boiling water with the sugar and shortening. Set aside until cool. Combine the yeast and the cold water. Beat in eggs. Combine mixtures. Finally add the flour and salt. Store covered in the refrigerator. Pinch off the dough as you want, and place in greased muffin tins. Let rise until double, and then bake at 375 degrees F. for 15 to 20 minutes.

—May Ward Maxwell
Columbia-Tusculum Historical District

Grandma's Easy Brown Bread

Yield: 6 loaves

5 cups graham flour	2 teaspoons salt
2 cups sour milk or buttermilk	1 12-ounce bottle blue label Karo
2 teaspoons soda	syrup

Preheat oven to 350 degrees F. Blend all of the ingredients. Grease six

146

20-ounce fruit cans and fill $^2/_3$ full. Bake about one hour. Remove from the cans after cooling.

—Dolores Daly
Hyde Park

> *To each and every artist,*
> *A synonym for cook,*
> *Who gave her choicest recipe*
> *And helped to make this book.*
> —The School of Housekeeping Cookbook, 1900

Minnie's Sage Bread

Ruth Clark's love of good cooking expressed itself in the fine collection of recipes in the *Log House Cookbook,* published by the Anderson Township Historical Society. This recipe was created by Minnie Sedler, Ruth's mother.

Yield: 2 large loaves or 5 very small ones

1 cup milk
3 tablespoons lard or shortening
3 tablespoons sugar
1 teaspoon salt
1 tablespoon sage leaves

2 tablespoons dried onions
1 cup warm water
2 packages dry yeast
4 cups white flour

Preheat the oven to 375 degrees F. Scald the milk. Add the lard, sugar, salt, sage, and onions. Set aside to cool. Dissolve the yeast in warm water and add to the cooled milk mixture. Add the flour and beat well. Then knead for three to five minutes. Set aside to rise until double, one to two hours depending on the warmth of the room. Place in greased loaf pans and let rise again for about one hour. Bake 35 to 40 minutes for large pans, 20 to 25 minutes for small pans.

—Ruth Clark
Anderson Township Historical Society

Strudel

This recipe makes enough dough for two strudels. Two favorite fillings follow, with precise measurements for one strudel each. There are scores of strudel recipes in Cincinnati, many excellent ones compiled by members of the Germania Society.

Dough

Yield: 2 strudels

½ cup milk
½ cup butter, at room temperature
½ cup sugar
½ teaspoon salt

2 packages dry yeast
½ cup warm water (115 degrees F.)
2 eggs, beaten until thick
4½ cups white flour, divided

Nuss Strudel (Nut Strudel)

½ cup honey
1 tablespoon butter
2½ cups walnuts, ground
Rind from one lemon

¼ teaspoon salt
Dash cinnamon
Evaporated milk

Apfel Strudel (Apple Strudel)

4 medium apples, peeled and sliced
   thin or shredded
¾ cup sugar

1 cup walnuts, ground
½ cup raisins
1 teaspoon cinnamon

Scald the milk, remove from heat, and add butter, sugar, and salt. In a large bowl dissolve the yeast in warm water. Stir in the milk mixture; add eggs and two of the cups of flour. Beat until smooth. Stir in the remaining flour until the dough comes away from the sides of the bowl. Knead the dough for 8 to 10 minutes. Cover the bowl with plastic wrap and set aside to rise in a warm place until double in size, about one hour. While the dough is rising, make the fillings.

For the nut strudel, heat together the honey and butter. Add the walnuts, lemon rind, salt, cinnamon, and enough evaporated milk to make it a spreading consistency. Mix well.

For the apple strudel, mix all of the ingredients together well.

When the dough has risen sufficiently, punch it down and divide it in half. Roll out one half of the dough on a lightly floured towel to a 10-by-14 inch rectangle. Spread with the filling, roll up tightly, seal the edges, and fold the ends. Place seam side down on a greased cookie sheet. Let it rise until double, about 30 minutes. Repeat for the second strudel. Bake until lightly browned at 350 degrees F. for 30 to 40 minutes.

—Helen Schwiegeraut
Grosbeck

Frittata

(Italian Egg Scramble)

This omelette is traditionally served by the Alfieri family on Easter morning after mass. They have quite a large feast; six of these omelettes are served (seventy-two eggs!) along with bacon, fruit salad, jello, hot wheat and egg breakfast rolls, orange juice, and coffee. For the adults there is also a double shot of anisette from a bottle stored only for this purpose and lasting through several years of the Easter toasts. As in the old country, asparagus is used in the frittata since it is the first spring vegetable and signifies new life.

Yield: 1 omelette; 6 to 8 servings

1 pound asparagus	1 dozen eggs
¼ cup chopped onion	Salt and pepper to taste
Bacon grease as needed	¼ cup Parmesan cheese

Cut the asparagus into bite-size pieces and steam until just tender. Using a 10-inch cast iron or teflon skillet, sauté the cooked asparagus and the onion in bacon grease measuring about ¼-inch in the bottom of the skillet. When the onions are transparent, beat the eggs. Beat in the salt, pepper, and cheese. Pour the egg mixture into the skillet and cook on a medium high heat (350 degrees F.), working the cooked eggs toward the center. Keep the egg moving until it has reached a semi-solid stage. Place a plate over the skillet and turn the skillet over until the eggs rest on the plate. Then slide the omelette off the plate back into the skillet to brown the other side. Cook another five minutes. Put the plate back on top of the omelette, flip the skillet over again until the omelette rests on the plate, and serve.

—Bob Alfieri

Tom Ward '67

The Cincinnati-based Delta Steamboat Company is the owner-operator of the steamboats Delta
Queen and Mississippi Queen. The Delta Queen, a venerable fifty-six years old, first operated
on overnight trips between Sacramento and San Francisco. After serving her country as a
U. S. Navy Yard Ferry Boat on San Francisco Bay during World War II, she was auctioned to
Tom Greene, then president of the Greene family's company. Captain Greene had her towed
across 5,000 miles of open sea to New Orleans, and then sailed her under her own power to
Pittsburg where she was remodeled and outfitted for passenger service. On June 30, 1948, she
made her maiden voyage on a round trip between Cincinnati and Cairo, Illinois. Because the
Delta Queen is an authentic, fully restored masterpiece, she was entered in the National Register
of Historic Places, June, 1970. Drawing by Tom Ward

Omelette Creole

This delectable recipe is served for breakfast aboard both the *Delta Queen* and the *Mississippi Queen* steamboats.

Yield: 1 serving

½ garlic clove, chopped fine
¼ onion, coarsely chopped
1 green onion, chopped fine
Sprig of parsley, chopped
Few drops olive oil
1 tomato, peeled and chopped

3 eggs
½ green pepper, chopped fine
Salt to taste
Dash cayenne
½ teaspoon gumbo filé

In a small skillet, sauté the garlic, onion, green onion, and parsley with the olive oil. Add the tomato and cook for a few minutes longer. Beat the eggs until light and fluffy. While beating, add green pepper, salt, pepper, and filé. Place the egg mixture in a prepared omelet pan and add half of the tomato mixture. Serve the other half on top of the omelette.

Big Dutch Baby

You'll need a heavy 12-inch skillet with a heatproof or removable handle for this mouth-watering, easy to make treat. You can make this huge pancake all for yourself or share it with a friend. In some homes it is called a German Oven Pancake.

Yield: 1 enormous pancake

Pancake

3 eggs
¾ cup milk
¾ cup white flour (or half
   whole wheat)

½ teaspoon salt
1½ tablespoons butter or margarine

Topping

2 tablespoons butter, melted
¼ cup confectioners' sugar

Lemon wedges for garnish

Preheat the oven to 450 degrees F. Beat together the eggs and milk. Add the flour and salt; beat until very smooth. Heat the butter in the skillet. As soon as it is melted and quite hot, pour in the batter and place the skillet into the oven. Bake for 15 minutes, then lower the temperature to 350 degrees F. and bake another ten minutes. During the first fifteen minutes of baking the pancake may puff up in large bubbles; pierce the biggest ones thoroughly with a fork. When the pancake is set and golden brown, bring it to the table in the skillet, top it with the melted butter, and sift confectioners' sugar over it. Cut pancake in halves or quarters. This is the classic version, served with lemon wedges.

Fancy Big Dutch Baby

Make the pancake as above, but do not serve the lemon wedges and make a filling instead.

Strawberry Filling

1 16-ounce box frozen strawberries

While the pancake is baking, prepare the filling. Heat the strawberries in a pan until completely defrosted and warm. Follow presentation below.

Apple Filling

1 pound tart apples	Cinnamon to taste
¼ cup melted butter or margarine	Nutmeg to taste
¼ cup sugar	

Core the apples and peel all or some of them. Slice thinly. Sauté the apples in the butter for about ten minutes and then add the sugar and spices. Turn off the heat. The apples should be tender but not too soft. When the pancake is ready, place it on an oval platter. Pour the filling on one side and fold it over. Pour over the melted butter, sprinkle with confectioners' sugar as above, and serve at once, slicing pieces off crosswise.

—Julia DuSablon

Goetta

Martha Finke Oehler of Covington, Kentucky claims that her ancestors "invented" goetta (pronounced get-ta) back around the turn of the century. The Finke family owned a large store and butchered meat regularly for the Covington Market at 6th and Main Streets near St. Patrick's. Similar to the Pennsylvania Dutch "scrapple," the goetta concoction was brought to the market but wasn't successful until the Finkes sold it as "Irish mush," or so the story goes. The goetta became popular and packages were transported across the Ohio River to Cincinnati markets where meat purveyors began selling their homemade versions in a German atmosphere. The word goetta doesn't appear in either German or Gaelic dictionaries, nor is the recipe found outside the greater Cincinnati vicinity. Goetta has been accepted by locals to mean "mush." The Finkes made the breakfast dish once a week in an iron kettle that held 100 pounds of meat; the remainder of the week the kettle was used to wash clothes. The Covington Municipal Historical Society has many of the Finke family artifacts at their new museum in Devou Park. To Martha's knowledge this seemingly original recipe was never written down, but contained an undisclosed and heretofore undiscovered secret ingredient. The following Crockpot Goetta recipe is a local favorite.

Crockpot Goetta

Yield: about 6 pounds

5 cups water
2½ cups pinhead oatmeal (rolled oats are not suitable)
3 teaspoons salt
½ teaspoon pepper
1 pound ground beef
1 pound ground pork or pork

sausage
1½ cups finely chopped onion
½ teaspoon sage
¼ teaspoon thyme
4 bay leaves
½ cup cornmeal to thicken

Place the water, oatmeal, salt, and pepper into a crockpot and mix well. Cook covered one hour on high, stirring two or three times. Add the beef and pork and break up well. Add the onion, sage, thyme, and bay leaves and cook for four hours on low, stirring occasionally. Uncover again, add the cornmeal, and cook another ½ hour uncovered. Spoon into two or three loaf pans and let cool. Chill and remove from the pans. Cut each loaf in half, wrap it in freezer paper or place it in plastic, and place one or two blocks in the refrigerator, freezing the remainder. Slice or form into patties. Dip in flour if desired. Fry in a small amount of hot fat. Do not allow the slices to touch in the skillet or they will run together. Brown each side until crusty.

Note: Hearty, delicious breakfast food with a couple of eggs, goetta is equally at home at the dinner table. As it fries, it leaves enough residue to make a good gravy.

Stovetop Goetta

Yield: approximately 6 pounds

3 quarts water
1 pound ground beef
1 pound ground pork
2 cups pinhead oatmeal (not rolled

oats)
1 medium onion, chopped fine
2 teaspoons salt
½ teaspoon pepper

Using your heaviest pan, place the ground meat in water, breaking up lumps while bringing the water to a boil. Add the remaining ingredients. Cook for one hour. Stir frequently; don't let it stick The goetta will be very thick when done. (Note: Some people declare the goetta done if a wooden spoon stands upright when stuck in the center of the pot.) Pour into loaf pans. Refrigerate. The goetta will be firm and can then be sliced and fried to a golden brown. Serve it with applesauce on top or with eggs at breakfast.

—Judy Deiters
Winton Place

Raised Doughnuts

Spending one month on board the towboat, one month at home, Rose Thompson has been a cook for the Ohio River Company for over twenty years. As she travels up and down the Ohio and Mississippi Rivers aboard the "barges" so familiar to Cincinnatians, she watches the sights go by from her galley window. She also cooks, from five o'clock in the morning until the last of the dozen crewmen has eaten supper. These doughnuts, one of her many specialties, usually disappear within twenty-four hours.

Yield: 6 dozen

Doughnuts

3 cups milk
4 tablespoons sugar
2 teaspoons salt
⅔ cup shortening (not oil)

2 eggs
4 packages yeast
8 cups white flour
Shortening for frying

154

Glaze

2 boxes confectioners' sugar	Water
2 tablespoons vanilla extract	

Heat the milk, sugar, salt and shortening until the shortening melts. Cool until warm. Add the eggs, yeast, and flour and mix well. Set aside to rise for about one hour. Roll the dough out on a floured table. Cut out doughnuts and let them rise one hour. While the dough is rising, mix together the glaze. Place the confectioners' sugar and vanilla in a bowl large enough to dip the doughnuts and add enough water to make the glaze a thickness like medium syrup. Drop the doughnuts in the hot shortening to fry at 350 degrees F. until golden brown. Flip at least once to brown on both sides. Next dip them in the glaze and lay them aside on wax paper to cool.

—Rose Thompson
Phillips Towboat

Doughnuts

One cup of sugar, one cup of milk,
Two eggs, beaten fine as silk,
Salt and nutmeg (lemon'll do)
Of baking powder, teaspoons two;
Lightly stir the flour in,
Roll on pieboard not too thin
Cut in diamonds, twists or rings,
Drop with care the doughy things
Into fat that briskly swells
Evenly the spongy cells.
Watch with care the time for turning
Fry them brown just short of burning.
Roll in sugar; serve when cool,
Price, a quarter for this rule.

I find the addition of a bit of butter or lard to be an improvement on the above recipe.

—Louis West
Christian Women's Missionary Cookbook, 1921

Fancy Egg Scramble

Most kitchens in our area respectfully acknowledge the culinary importance of both chicken and egg. Egg cups, milk glass egg bowls, chicken soup tureens, egg baskets, and hen and rooster salt and pepper shakers are collected. A favorite craft was knitting the egg "cosy," a small woolen chicken that "sat" atop the egg in an egg cup. At Easter time the rabbit cosy was in vogue. For large breakfasts, lunches, or late suppers where individual servings are impractical, an egg casserole is always welcomed.

Yield: 12 servings

Cheese Sauce

2 tablespoons butter or margarine
2 tablespoons flour
2 cups milk

1½ cups grated cheese of choice
Salt and pepper to taste

Scramble

1 cup chopped Canadian bacon
  or ham
¼ cup chopped green onion
7 tablespoons butter or margarine,
  divided

12 eggs
1 3-ounce can mushrooms, drained
2½ cups soft breadcrumbs (3 slices)
⅛ teaspoon paprika

To make the cheese sauce, melt the butter in a saucepan, add the flour, and stir well. Let it bubble a few minutes, add the milk, and stir until

156

smooth and thickened. Turn off the heat. Add the cheese and stir well. Season with salt and pepper and set aside.

In a large skillet sauté the bacon or ham and onion in 3 tablespoons of the butter until the onion is soft. Beat the eggs. Add the eggs and mushrooms to the skillet, scrambling until just set. Fold the egg mixture into the cheese sauce. Pour it into a greased 12-by-7-by-2 inch baking dish. Melt the remaining 4 tablespoons of butter and combine with the breadcrumbs and paprika. Sprinkle atop the eggs. Cover. Chill at least thirty minutes or overnight before serving. Bake uncovered at 350 degrees F. for thirty minutes.

—Mary Joseph Maxwell
Columbia-Tusculum Historical District

Buttermilk Pancakes

Grandma loved her glass of buttermilk while she enjoyed a rest in a backyard lawn chair under a willow tree. She sipped it cold, right out of the icebox, with a little salt and pepper on top. Most people take their buttermilk in pancakes nowadays. The secret is to "age" the batter, preparing it the day before.

Yield: 16 4-inch pancakes

1 egg
1¼ cups buttermilk
2 tablespoons salad oil or soft
   shortening
1¼ cups flour

1 teaspoon sugar
1 teaspoon baking powder
½ teaspoon baking soda
½ teaspoon salt

Beat the egg thoroughly, and then beat in the remaining ingredients. Blend with a rotary beater until smooth. When ready to bake the pancakes, lightly grease a griddle or skillet and heat it up slowly. The griddle is ready when a drop of water "skitters" around. Pour the batter from the tip of a large spoon into circles. As soon as they are puffed and full of bubbles turn and brown on the other side. Serve with butter and pure maple syrup or jelly.

—Justine Rolston
Sharonville

157

Recipe for an Appetite

My lad, who sits at breakfast
  With forehead in a frown,
Because the chop is under-done
  And the fritter over-brown.

Just leave your dainty mincing,
  And take, to mend your fare,
A slice of golden sunshine,
  And a cup of the morning air.

And when you have eat and drunken,
  If you want a little fun,
Throw by your jacket of broadcloth,
  And take an up-hill run.

And what with one and the other
  You will be so strong and gay,
That work will be only a pleasure
  Through all the rest of the day.

And when it is time for supper,
  Your bread and milk will be
As sweet as a comb of honey.
  Will you try my recipe?

—Alice and Phoebe Cary's Poems, 1865

Liver Pudding and Oatmeal Sausage

The best method to make these locally produced treats is to place a little water in a skillet, add the sausage of your choice, and then steam on low heat for at least half an hour, covered. Turn occasionally, but do not pierce with a fork. When the water has evaporated, add a small amount of oil or a strip of bacon and then brown the sausage on all sides, using a medium heat. Singe until the skin pops and cracks open, then cook a few minutes longer. Remove to a plate and serve with eggs for breakfast or with vegetables for dinner.

Note: The rich and slightly exotic blood sausage (in olden days called "johnny-in-the-bag") is cooked in the same manner. Some prefer not to allow the skin to break open during cooking but bring the sausage to the table whole, where the contents will spill forth when first touched with the fork.

—Chip Bare, Bare's Meats
Findlay Market

Stewed Fruit

This is best if made the night before and left standing on the stove until morning. Serve at room temperature.

Yield: 1 serving

3 dried prunes
2 dried figs
2 dried peaches or apricots

Handful of raisins
Cinnamon (optional)

Place ingredients into a pan and cover with water. Add a dash or two of cinnamon if you desire, or if you're making a large batch, a cinnamon stick. Bring to a boil, and then simmer for 30 to 45 minutes covered. Take care that the syrup gets slightly thickened but does not boil off. Add more water if necessary.

—Joann Jones
Elmwood Place

Eggs and Brains

This old family recipe came from Thomas Howard Maxwell whose ancestry was thought to have been Scottish.

Buy a little meat tray of brains and soak them in cold water, pouring the water off and putting fresh water on them until the water is clear. Nowadays they are really not as bloody as they used to be. After they are soaked, pull off the membrane with a sharp knife. This comes off easily; in other words they are pretty cleaned up by the time they get to the meat case. After they are clean, cut them into small pieces. Flour and season and fry in oil until they are fluffy and dry when broken with a fork. Set aside. Scramble eggs in butter and add the brains, stirring them around in the skillet as the eggs are cooking. Serve on a platter with a sprinkling of paprika on top.

—Bernadette Martin

159

McMicken Hall-University of Cincinnati. This beautiful red brick building houses the College of Arts and Sciences on campus. One of the important developments the university provided society is the co-op system of education, whereby students alternate working experience and class attendance. Another innovative move was the choice to use a public hospital as a medical-teaching facility. The Golden Gate Bridge in San Francisco and the Pan Am Building in New York were designed by UC graduates. The Sabin vaccine for polio was discovered at UC, likewise the first method of making safe a marketable no-knock gasoline. Drawing by Charles Kelsch, courtesy Row House Gallery, Milford

Breakfast Muffins

Everyone has a never-fail recipe for homemade muffins using flour and sugar, but here is one that uses the "natural" ingredients so popular in today's cooking. It is a free-style recipe; you can substitute what you have on hand to a certain degree, and measurements need not be totally exact.

Yield: 18 muffins

1-1/2 cups milk or fruit juice
1/2 cup salad oil
1/4 cup honey or maple syrup
1 to 2 eggs, depending on size
3 cups wheat flour (or any combination of flours)
1 tablespoon baking powder

1/2 teaspoon salt
1/2 cup wheat germ, oats, or dry cereal
1/2 cup raisins (optional)
1/4 cup chopped nuts (optional)
1 apple, chopped (optional)

Preheat oven to 350 degrees F. Beat together the milk or juice, oil, honey or syrup and eggs. Sift the flour, baking powder and salt into the liquid ingredients, add the wheat germ (etc.) and any optionals, and stir only to moisten. Spoon batter into greased muffin tins and bake for 20 minutes. Break and eat with a patty of butter inside.

—Charles DuSablon
University of Cincinnati

Winter, 1945

On very cold winter mornings, before the coal furnace was stoked up in the basement, my mother would run down to the kitchen from her bedroom, turn on the gas burners for a few minutes and preheat the oven for a coffeecake. After the batter was in the oven she'd call us kids for school. We could hear her then, in the basement loading wood and a few pieces of newspaper into the silver painted cavern with the squeaky hinged door, coaxing the fire to catch. Eventually she would place a large lump or two of coal on the flames and race back up to the warming kitchen. When the coffeecake was done she would open the oven door wide and hang our socks along the opening, weighing the ends down with her iron skillets. We sissy children didn't dress in our cold bedroom, we grabbed our clothes and headed for that kitchen as fast as our bare feet would carry us. We went off to school those days with rosy cheeks, toasty stockings and warm coffeecake in our tummies.

—Clermont Country *Newsletter,* 1981

The Skyline of Cincinnati in 1945. The Provident Bank Tower is on the left; the Carew Tower to the right is Cincinnati's tallest building since 1930, with forty-nine floors and an observation deck. Drawing by Edward Timothy Hurley

Eggs n' Chard

A great number of Cincinnati area gardeners make room between the roses and marigolds for some vegetable plants: tomatoes, certainly, leaf lettuce, green onions, radishes, and frequently Swiss chard. Nothing can compare to rising on a bright summer morning, going to the garden, and picking the chard, a few onions, and a tomato or two for breakfast! In olden days (and even now in county backyards) a trip to the henhouse was also in order.

Yield: 2 servings

4 cups chopped Swiss chard
  or spinach
3 tablespoons butter or salad oil
2 green onions
4 large eggs

1 tablespoon milk
Salt to taste
Freshly ground pepper
Parmesan cheese for garnish
Sliced tomato for garnish

162

Fill a basin with cold water and drop in the chard. Swish it around to wash; drain, and repeat if necessary. Chop roughly, a little more or less in the measuring cup won't make any difference. Place in a skillet and heat on a low flame, covered. There should be enough water left on the leaves to wilt them; if not, add a tablespoon of water. When the chard is wilted, add the butter and green onions and sauté everything for about three minutes. Beat the eggs and milk together. Turn up the heat and add the egg mixture to the chard mixture and scramble quickly. Remove to two serving plates, add salt and pepper to taste. Sprinkle with Parmesan cheese and serve with tomato slices.

—Sean Bailey
Loveland

Cornbread Stew

The Jesuits in the Midwest had their origins in a Missouri farm community where they arose at five in the morning, did chores, and ate breakfast about 7:15. Thus, it was necessary to appease these hearty appetites. Although this particular recipe was originally served as a breakfast in the old days, it has become a traditional lunch served family style at retreats. Chef Bob boasts that the men "really look forward to it."

Yield: 6 servings

1½ pounds beef, cubed
¼ cup flour
¼ cup salad oil
2 beef bouillon cubes
2 bay leaves
1 tablespoon lemon juice
Dash or two allspice
Salt and pepper to taste
6 potatoes, quartered

6 medium onions, quartered
6 carrots, cut in chunks
6 stalks celery, cut in chunks
Tomatoes (optional)
1 9-inch pan cornbread (prepared during the final cooking of the stew)
Butter as needed
Syrup as needed

Dredge the beef in the flour and then brown slowly on all sides in oil in a stewpot. Add about a quart of water, the bouillon cubes, bay leaf, lemon juice, allspice, salt, and pepper. Cover and simmer at least two hours. Taste and adjust the seasonings. Then add the vegetables, cover, and continue cooking until they are fork tender, about 15 minutes. Place a

163

chunk of hot buttered cornbread in the bottom of a dish, cover with syrup if desired, then add the stew, and serve.

—Brother Robert Cardosi, S.J.
Chef-Manager, Jesuit Community Kitchen,
Xavier University

Desserts

Chocolate Dipped Strawberries

Yield: Depends solely on the size of the berries

1 quart strawberries
8 ounces white chocolate or semi-sweet chocolate

Wash the strawberries and drain on paper towels until dry. Using a double boiler, melt the chocolate over hot, not boiling, water. Insert a toothpick into the stem end of a berry. Dip into chocolate; lift out quickly. Allow excess to run off. Place on waxed paper. Cool 15 minutes or until firm. The berries may be refrigerated several hours.

—Aichholz Farm

Plum Dumplings

(Zwetschken Knodel)

Many Cincinnati babies are affectionately called "dumplin's" because, like this favorite dessert, they're soft and pleasing.

Yield: 2 dozen

6 or 7 medium potatoes (1⅔ pound)	24 fresh blue damson plums
1 teaspoon salt	4 tablespoons butter
1 egg	½ cup breadcrumbs
2 cups flour	⅓ cup sugar

Boil the potatoes in the skin. While still hot, peel and force them through a ricer or strainer onto a board. Pile in a mound with a depression in the center. Sprinkle salt on the potatoes and drop the egg in the depression. Cover with potato and mix well with the hands. Pour the flour over the potatoes and mix and knead in until you have a dough that can be handled, about five minutes. Form into a sausage about 2½ inches in diameter. Wash the plums and dry thoroughly. Cut a ¾-inch slice of the potato roll and roll it around a plum (do not remove the pit) so that the plum is completely and evenly covered. If preferred, peel the plums first. Cook the dumplings in a covered kettle of boiling, salted water for five minutes. Melt the butter, add crumbs and sugar, and brown very slightly. Add the boiling dumplings and gently coat them with the mixture. Serve hot.

—Mrs. Walter Mueller
Recipes, 1952

Poppyseed Cake

Uncle Al and Captain Wendy have thrilled youngsters in the greater Cincinnati area for thirty-three years, appearing live every weekday morning on WCPO-TV and at innumerable festivities and functions. "Uncle Al Town" has become a distinct part of family life in this town; Al and Wanda share this recipe, a favorite one with the Lewis family.

Cake

¾ cup poppyseeds
¾ cup milk
¾ cup butter or shortening, at room temperature
1½ cups sugar

2 cups sifted cake flour
2 teaspoons baking powder
4 teaspoons vanilla extract
5 egg whites, stiffly beaten

Sweet Butter Frosting

¾ cup sugar
3 tablespoons flour
1 egg
1 cup milk

1 cup (2 sticks) butter, at room temperature
2 tablespoons confectioners' sugar
1 teaspoon vanilla extract

Soak the poppyseeds in the milk for at least six hours or overnight. When ready to assemble the cake, preheat the oven to 375 degrees F. Cream the butter and sugar, add the poppyseed mixture alternately with the flour and baking powder, and beat well. Add the vanilla, and then fold in the egg whites. Bake in two 8 or 9-inch greased and floured cake pans for 20 or 30 minutes. Do not open the oven for the first twenty minutes.

To make the frosting, mix the sugar and flour, add the egg, and beat well. Add the milk and cook in a double boiler until thickened. Cool completely. Cream the butter and sugar; add to the first mixture. Beat with an electric mixer until it is like whipped cream. Add vanilla. Frost the cake when cool.

—Wanda Lewis

Catharine Esther Beecher, sister of author Harriet Beecher Stowe, lived in Cincinnati for about ten years. Her great interest was making housework easier for women so that they could spend more time on their education. She authored many domestic books including a Treatise on Domestic Economy *and its supplement.* Miss Beecher's Domestic Receipt-Book. *From the latter book, published by Harper and Bros. in 1868, come the following delightful receipts:*

Little Girl's Pie

Take a deep dish, the size of a soup plate, fill it, heaping, with peeled tart apples, cored and quartered; pour over it one tea-cup of molasses, and three great spoonfuls of sugar, dredge over this a considerable quantity of flour, enough to thicken the syrup a great deal. Cover it with a crust made of cream, if you have it, if not, common dough, with butter worked in, or plain pie crust, and lap the edge over the dish, and pinch it down tight, to keep the syrup from running out. Bake about an hour and a half. Make several at once, as they keep well.

Little Boy's Pudding

One tea-cup of rice
One tea-cup of sugar
One half tea-cup of butter

One quart of milk
Nutmeg, cinnamon, and salt to
   the taste

Put the butter in melted, and mix all in a pudding dish, and bake it two hours, stirring it frequently, until the rice is swollen.
This is good made without butter.

Blackberry Cake with Caramel Icing

Mary prefers using blackberry preserves to make this popular cake, but you can use blackberry jam if you don't mind the seeds. It was made in the old days using homegrown, home preserved blackberries, and blending the fresh or preserved berries first is a satisfying touch.

1 cup shortening or margarine
2 cups sugar
4 eggs, separated
1 cup sour milk or buttermilk
3 cups flour
½ teaspoon baking soda
3 teaspoons baking powder

Pinch salt
2 teaspoons cinnamon
½ teaspoon nutmeg
¼ teaspoon allspice
¼ teaspoon ground cloves
2 cups blackberries or 1-1½ cups
   preserves or jam

Caramel Icing

2 cups light brown sugar
½ cup (1 stick) butter or margarine

½ cup half and half cream
1 teaspoon vanilla extract

Preheat oven to 350 degrees F. Cream together the shortening and sugar. Add the egg yolks and beat well. Stir in the sour milk. Sift the flour twice, then sift together the flour, soda, baking powder, and salt, adding them to the liquid ingredients. Stir in the spices. Then stir in the blackberries or preserves. Beat the egg whites until stiff and fold them into the batter. Pour into three 8-inch greased and floured pans. Bake 30 to 45 minutes. Test with the clean end of a broomstraw for doneness.

When the cake is cool and ready to ice, combine the sugar, butter and half and half in a heavy skillet. Place on low heat, bringing slowly to a boil, mixing until smooth. Boil until thick and waxy, about three minutes, without stirring. Remove from heat, add the vanilla, stir, then beat until thick enough to spread. Soft and delicious to the last bite, this icing never gets hard even if the cake gets stale. (If icing gets too thick, thin with half and half.)

—Mary Rose Pitzer
Mt. Washington

The River Downs Race Track opened in 1925 and operated on and off until 1937, when it had to be rebuilt after the flood. Exciting thoroughbred racing is available at this ever popular race track. Drawing by Geneva South

Bread Pudding with Whiskey Sauce

Lou Moses, a thirty-five-year veteran of the hospitality industry and director of hotel services for the *Mississippi Queen* and the *Delta Queen*, was born in Holland. He received his professional training in the Netherlands and served apprenticeships at the Grand Hotel Scheveningen and Metrople in Brussels. He was a steward aboard the "Etoile du Nord," the luxury train between Paris and Amsterdam, a cook at the Sharon Hotel in Israel, *chef garde* manger at New York's Mayfair Hotel, and *maitre d'* at Tode's Inn in Ridgefield, Connecticut. Lou shares this recipe.

Yield: 12 to 15 servings

1 loaf stale bread	2 tablespoons vanilla extract
1 quart milk	1 cup raisins
4 eggs	2 apples, peeled, cored, and sliced
2 cups sugar	4 tablespoons butter

Whiskey Sauce

½ cup (1 stick) butter, melted	1 egg, beaten
1 cup sugar	Whiskey to taste

Preheat oven to 350 degrees F. Crush the bread into the milk and mix well. Beat the eggs and add to the bread and milk, together with the sugar, vanilla, raisins, and apples. Mix well. Melt the butter in the pan in which you're going to bake the pudding, and then pour in the rest of the

170

ingredients. Bake about 50 minutes, or until the pudding is firm. This can be served as is, or with the Whiskey Sauce.

To make the sauce, cream the butter and sugar in a double boiler over a medium heat. Add the egg and stir rapidly so that the egg doesn't curdle. When well mixed, allow to cool. Add whiskey to taste (a jigger or two). Bon appetit!

Dump Cake

This contributor was a Cincinnati fireman for thirty-five years, and this was a favorite firehouse recipe. One box of cake mix will make two of these concoctions.

Yield: 1 8-inch cake

1 21-ounce can cherry pie filling
1 13-ounce can pineapple tidbits
Shredded coconut as needed

2 cups yellow cake mix
Margarine as needed

Preheat oven to 350 degrees F. Pour the cherries into an ungreased 8-inch cake pan. Pour the pineapple evenly over the cherries. Cover with coconut. Sprinkle on the cake mix. Place thin pats of margarine over the entire surface of the cake mix. Bake for 50 to 60 minutes or until the top is golden brown.

—Henry Wolfer
District 5
Cincinnati Fire Department

Spongecake

This cake is good for making fruit-filled shortcakes, ice cream cakes, or any kind of dessert that calls for spongecake or ladyfingers. It is also good frosted with a white or orange icing or sprinkled with confectioners' sugar for a light, easily digested dessert.

Yield: 1 large cake

6 eggs, separated
¾ teaspoon cream of tartar
1½ cups sugar, divided
⅓ cup orange juice or cold water

¼ teaspoon salt
1 teaspoon vanilla extract
1½ cups cake flour
½ teaspoon baking powder

Preheat oven to 350 degrees F. In a large bowl, beat the egg whites until frothy. Add the cream of tartar and continue beating on high speed until stiff. Slowly beat in one half cup of the sugar. In another bowl beat the egg yolks until lemon colored. Add the orange juice or water and beat vigorously. Add the remaining sugar slowly. Continue beating; beat in the salt and vanilla. Sift the cake flour with the baking powder and stir slowly into the egg yolks; fold in the egg whites. Turn batter gently into an ungreased, floured tube pan or 10-inch springform pan. Bake for one hour, fifteen minutes. Remove from oven and cool upside down on a cake rack or soda pop bottle.

—Elsie Firstos

Carrot Cake

This is one of the favorite desserts in America today. Making this version is easier than going to the store to buy it ready-made.

Yield: 1 large cake

1 cup salad oil	1 teaspoon cinnamon
4 eggs	1 teaspoon salt
1-1/2 cups sugar (or half honey)	1-1/2 teaspoons baking soda
3 cups carrots, chopped into 1-inch pieces	1 7-ounce can crushed pineapple, well drained (optional)
2 cups white flour (or half whole wheat)	1/2 cup nuts, chopped (optional)
2 teaspoons baking powder	raisins (optional)

Icing

4 ounces cream cheese, at room temperature	1/2 cup confectioners' sugar or honey
4 tablespoons butter, at room temperature	1 teaspoon vanilla extract

Preheat oven to 350 degrees F. Combine the oil and eggs in a blender; add the sugar gradually. Then add the carrot chunks, a few at a time, allowing them to blend nicely into the mixture. Remove the carrot mixture from the blender into a bowl. Sift together and add the remaining ingredients, stirring well. Pour into a greased 9-by-13-inch pan, or a 10-inch tube pan; tap on counter to release bubbles. Bake for 45 to 50 minutes. Cool cake in pan.

For the icing, mix the ingredients together, adjusting to suit your own taste. Ice cake right in the pan and cut into squares; or, remove tube cake and glaze with 1/2 cup confectioners' sugar and 1/4 cup lemon juice.

—Dorinda Maxwell
Point Pleasant

172

Maraschino Cherry Cake

This old cake recipe is a forerunner to the red food-colored versions so popular today. It is dramatic and delicious.

Yield: 1 tube cake

2 5-ounce bottles maraschino
  cherries
Milk as needed
¼ pound walnut or pecan pieces
3¼ cups flour, divided
1 cup (2 sticks) butter, at room

temperature
2 cups sugar
4 eggs, separated
1 teaspoon baking soda
2 teaspoons baking powder

Preheat oven to 350 degrees F. Reserving the juice, drain and chop the cherries. Pour the cherry juice in a cup and fill with milk to measure one cup. Place the cherries and nuts in a bowl. Sprinkle ¼ cup of the flour over the cherries and nuts. Cream the butter and sugar thoroughly, adding the egg yolks one by one, beating well. Add the cherries and nuts. Sift the remaining three cups of flour with the baking soda and baking powder and add alternately with the liquid to the butter mixture. Beat the egg whites until stiff and fold them into the mixture. Bake in a greased fluted tube pan for one hour.

Pound Cake

(Bund Kuchen)

The proud owner of this old cookbook selected the following recipe since it is similar to a cake her husband's mother made. The undated cookbook is a priceless possession, probably dating back to before the turn of the century.

One penny cake of yeast, 1 teaspoon sugar, 1 half glass lukewarm water, let rise. Stir in two cups of warm milk and flour enough to make a batter. Let rise one-half hour, keep covered. Cream with hands one cup sugar, one-fourth pound butter, add four eggs, beaten separately. Grated lemon rind, salt and 4 tablespoons flour. Fill pan half full, let rise three-fourths of an hour. Put in hot oven and don't open until fifteen minutes then lower the heat and bake one hour. (Lulu Schmittenhenner, Northside)

—Velma Eydel
from Choice Cookery, *circa 1900*

Alexander Koehler

1877

		$	
Spt 3	Cider		15
	Whiskey		10
	Nary		10
	Lace		14
17	1 ft Molasses		10
21	Buttons		5
	Crackers		10
	Drilling		3
24	pr Stim		2
	Buttons		20
	Muslins		65
	Comb		10
	Bees		25
25	1 Bolt Braid		10
	Buttons		3
	Jelly Glasses		12
26	6 Yrd Flannel	1	50
30	1 Gall. Oil		20
30	Beef		20
	Vinger		9
	Red Flannel 2½ yrd		63
	Yeast		5
Oct 1	Seling wax		5
	3 W Nail		15
2	1 Gall Vinegar		30
	1 W Coffee		30
8	2 W Sugar		25
	Beef		10
		$ 6.06	
Oct 23	Cash for Butter	2.12	
	By Ballence Due	# 4 14	
	Ving Ballence	# 93	
	Mustard Seed		5
10 g	Washing soda		48
1 ft Lime		10
25	2 W Slised Ham		35
	3 qt Peas		25
	1 W Crackers		10
	Barley		10
	Nut Megs		10
	Ex. Coffee		10
	4 Yrd Calico		28
26	Drilling		15
	Buttons		3
	Coal Oil		20
Brought Over No 228	$ 71	

From the ledger of the Linnemann Dry Goods and General Store on Kellogg Pike in California. The Koehler and Linnemann families were among those thousands of German immigrants who settled the area in the early 1800s. The original store building still stands and is currently in use as a bar.

Irish Applesauce Cake

It is a proven fact in Cincinnati that many good marriages come from the mixture of Irish and German heritage. This recipe comes from Bridgetown where there are many such marriages!

Yield: 1 sheet cake

3 cups flour
¾ cup sugar
½ teaspoon salt
3 egg yolks
1 cup (2 sticks) butter, at room temperature

Grated rind of one lemon
1 pound jar or can applesauce (1¾ cup)
½ teaspoon cinnamon
¼ teaspoon ground cloves

Preheat oven to 350 degrees F. Mix the flour, sugar, salt, egg yolks, butter, and lemon rind. Divide the mixture in two parts; press one part into the bottom of a greased 9-by-13-inch pan. Mix the applesauce, cinnamon, and cloves. Spread over the dough in the pan. Place the rest of the dough over the applesauce. Bake until cake tester comes out dry. Serve plain or topped with whipped cream or a lemon sauce.

—Ervin and Pat (O'Brien) Mueller
Bridgetown

Nut Torte

(Nusstorte)

Yield: 16 to 20 servings

Torte

1½ cups sugar
5 eggs, separated and 1 whole egg
2½ cups finely ground hazelnuts or walnuts
3 tablespoons cornstarch

Fine dry bread or cake crumbs
2 cups whipped cream
Vanilla extract or dark rum to taste
Confectioners' sugar to taste
Grated semi-sweet chocolate

Mocha Cream Filling

½ cup strong black coffee
4 egg yolks
¾ cup sugar

½ teaspoon cornstarch
1 cup butter (sweet, unsalted preferred)

Preheat oven to 350 degrees F. Add the sugar to a large bowl of electric mixer. Beat the five egg yolks and one whole egg until foamy, add to the sugar, and beat at high speed until thickened and pale yellow. Mix together the nuts and cornstarch; fold into the egg mixture. Wash and dry the beaters, and then beat the egg whites (now at room temperature for best volume) until stiff. Fold gently into the nut and egg mixture. Sprinkle two greased 9-inch round cake pans with the crumbs and divide the batter between them. Bake for about 30 minutes or until lightly browned and set throughout. Meanwhile, add vanilla (or rum) and confectioners' sugar to whipped cream as desired.

Cool the tortes 10 minutes on cake racks, remove from pans, and cool thoroughly. Cut each layer into three layers, crosswise, with a serrated knife. To make this easier, place the layers on a cookie sheet, cover with waxed paper, and freeze until nearly firm.

To prepare the Mocha Cream Filling, beat the coffee, egg yolks, sugar, and cornstarch in the top of a double boiler until thickened. Stir with a wooden spoon or wire whisk. Cool. Beat the butter with an electric mixer until creamy. Gradually add the cooked coffee mixture to the butter. Whip until smooth and thick. Set aside.

To assemble, place one thin layer of Nusstorte on a serving plate and spread the top with mocha cream. Top with another layer and spread with whipped cream. Continue adding layers and alternating the fillings, six layers in all. Frost the sides with whipped cream. Decorate with grated semi-sweet chocolate.

Note: The torte freezes well. To serve remove from freezer during the morning of serving day and place in the refrigerator until ready to serve.

—Elsie Firstos
Westwood

Graham Nut Cake with Lemon Icing

This old cake recipe may date as far back as the graham cracker. It is surprisingly moist and rich, even without the icing.

Yield: 2 9-inch layers

40 graham cracker squares, crushed
1½ cups sugar
1 tablespoon baking powder

1½ cups milk
2 eggs, beaten
1 tablespoon butter, melted (or oil)
1 cup black walnuts, broken

Icing

⅓ cup butter, at room temperature
3 cups confectioners' sugar
3 tablespoons lemon juice

1½ tablespoons lemon rind, grated
1 egg yolk (optional)

Preheat oven to 350 degrees F. Mix the crushed grahams, sugar, and baking powder together in a bowl. Add the milk, eggs, and butter and blend well. Stir in the walnuts. Place in two greased 9-inch baking pans, or a 9-by-13-inch baking dish and bake for 25 to 30 minutes. Cool and frost.

To make Lemon Icing, blend together the butter and sugar until smooth, add the lemon juice, rind, and egg yolk. Stir until very smooth.

—Maey Schott
Western Hills

Viennese Meringue Torte

Vienna, a city known for its many pastry shops, is the original home of this widely known torte. It is a large cake, suitable for festive occasions. Lottie Wilton was born in Vienna and came to Cincinnati in 1939 bringing with her a collection of incredible Viennese cookbooks.

Yield: 1 torte

9 egg whites
½ pound confectioners' sugar, sifted
½ pound almonds, pecans, or
   walnuts, chopped very fine
¼ pound candied fruit, figs, dates,

chopped very fine. (Some of the
fruit should be red and green for a
holiday effect.)
10 vanilla wafers, crushed

Preheat oven to 300 degrees F. Beat the egg whites stiff. Slowly add the sifted sugar, beating all the while. Gradually fold in the chopped nuts, fruit, and vanilla wafer crumbs. Grease a spring form pan and dust it lightly with flour. Spoon in the mixture. Bake for about 45 minutes. The torte is finished when the cake tester comes out dry. Turn off the oven, open the oven door, and let the torte cool inside the open oven for 30 minutes. Remove. Cool completely before serving. You can make this torte in advance and keep it for a couple of days in the freezer, well wrapped in aluminum foil. Have it completely at room temperature before serving. To make it very festive, top with a layer of whipped cream and a circle of maraschino cherries.

—Charlotte Wilton
Madisonville

Glendale Depot. Just off the village square in Glendale stands this most important building which replaced the original structure shortly after it was destroyed by fire in 1880. Except for the presence of a small railroad switching-station crew, it is now vacant. Drawing by Geneva South

Mince Meat

Two pounds beef, two pounds currants, two pounds raisins, two pounds beef suet, one pound citron, one and one-half pounds candied lemon peel, four pounds apples, two pounds sugar, two grated nutmegs, one-fourth ounce cloves, one-fourth ounce mase, one-half ounce cinnamon, one teaspoon salt, two lemons, juice and rind; two oranges, juice and rind. Simmer the meat gently till tender, and when cold chop apples and suet. Mix the dry ingredients, then add juice and rinds of oranges and lemons. Pack in a stone jar, cover close and keep cool. This meat will keep all winter. Cider can be added if so desired.

—Mrs. W. T. Berry
Tried and . . . True, 1900

178

Cream Cheesecake

New York has nothing on Cincinnati when it comes to cheesecake. Sold in bakeries throughout the city and in restaurants from Frisch's to the Maisonette, this mouthwatering dessert comes in two classic versions: cream cheese and cottage (dry) cheese.

Yield: 1 9-inch cake

2 8-ounce packages cream cheese, at room temperature
⅔ cup sugar
3 eggs
1 teaspoon almond extract

1 teaspoon lemon juice
½ pint sour cream
3 tablespoons sugar
1 teaspoon vanilla extract

Preheat oven to 350 degrees F. Blend together the cream cheese and sugar. With a mixer beat in the eggs, and then beat the mixture for a few minutes on high. Add the almond extract and lemon juice and beat until light and fluffy. Pour into a well-greased 9-inch *glass* pie dish. Bake for 35 minutes. Cool 15 minutes. While the cake is cooling, mix the sour cream, sugar, and vanilla. Spread atop the cake and return to the oven for 5 minutes to set the mixture. Serve cold.

—Dolores Whitson
Milford

Old German Cheesecake

The donor of this classic recipe, which originated in an old German cookbook, cautions that although the dough is set aside to rise, you won't detect much of a billowing in size. It's just the nature of this crust.

Yield: 2 cheesecakes

Crust

½ cup milk, scalded
1 package yeast, dry or compressed
½ cup sugar
1 egg, beaten

½ teaspoon salt
2½ cups flour
2 tablespoons butter, melted

Filling

4 eggs, separated	2 tablespoons flour
1 cup sugar	¾ cup milk
4 cups cottage cheese (some prefer it whipped)	½ teaspoon almond extract
	1 teaspoon vanilla extract

To prepare the dough, scald the milk and then cool it to lukewarm. Pour it over the yeast and stir well. Add the sugar, beaten egg, salt, and flour; stir well. Add the melted butter. Knead until a smooth dough is formed. Place in a greased bowl and set aside to rise 1½ hours. Knead again, divide in half, round up, and cover. Let stand on a floured board for 45 minutes. Roll out, stretch, and roll out again until each round fits an 8 or 9-inch greased and floured cake pan. Place in the pans but don't allow the dough to shrink away from the sides.

Preheat oven to 325 degrees F. To make the filling, beat the egg yolks well, and then beat in the sugar. Fold in the cheese, flour, and milk. Fold in the stiffly beaten egg whites, almond extract, and vanilla. Pour into the dough-lined pans and bake 1½ hours. Cool in pans.

—Velma Eydel
Westwood

Cincinnati Cake

This very, very old recipe was printed in a cookbook long before the turn of the century. The cookbook belonged to the grandmother of the donor and was thought to have originated either in Mississippi or Louisville, Kentucky. Grandma had seven boys, all of whom she taught to cook. The book was thought to have been her "married" cookbook. It was in bad shape when Marion jotted down some of the recipes and unfortunately may have inadvertently been thrown away.

> *Pour over one pound fat salt pork, chopped fine and free from lean and rind, one pint boiling water, let stand until nearly cold; add two cups brown sugar, one of molasses, one tablespoon each of cloves and nutmeg, and two of cinnamon, two pounds raisins, fourth pound citron, half glass brandy, three teaspoons of baking powder, and seven cups of sifted flour. Bake 2½ hours. This is excellent, and requires neither butter nor eggs.*

Note: A similar cake titled "War Cake" appeared in a 1917 publication entitled the *Liberty Cook Book* published by the Cincinnati's Woman's Club.

—Marion Memke
Madisonville

Aunt Caroline's Coca-Cola Cake

Cincinnatians love their Ohio River, and they deviously piece together hours to spend boating, water skiing, and picnicking at water's edge. When the families get together at their riverside trailers, colored lanterns glowing, Tripoli cards being shuffled—this is the dessert that is asked for.

Yield: 1 sheet cake

2 cups sugar
2 cups flour
½ cup salad oil
3 tablespoons cocoa powder
½ cup (1 stick) butter
1 cup Coca-Cola

½ cup buttermilk
1 teaspoon baking soda
1 teaspoon vanilla extract
2 eggs
1½ cups miniature marshmallows

Icing

4 tablespoons butter
4 teaspoons cocoa powder
3 tablespoons Coca-Cola
½ box (½ pound) confectioners'

sugar
½ teaspoon vanilla extract
½ cup chopped nuts

Preheat oven to 350 degrees F. Sift sugar and flour together into a mixing bowl. Place oil, cocoa, butter and cola in a saucepan; mix and bring to a boil. Pour the boiling mixture over the flour and sugar and beat well. Add the remaining ingredients and mix well. (Marshmallows do not liquify; batter will be thin.) Pour into a greased and floured 9-by-13-inch baking dish or pan and bake for 45 minutes. Cool.

For the icing, place the butter, cocoa, and cola in a saucepan and bring to a boil. Remove from heat and add confectioners' sugar, vanilla, and nuts. Mix well. Spread on the cake while the mixture is still warm.

—Caroline Maxwell
East End

Ice Cream Dessert

This sinful sweet features Cincinnati's one and only Graeter's, which many believe to be the world's finest ice cream. It is not only the egg, cream and homemade chocolate that makes it so superior; their French pot freezing technique gives it a smooth and voluptuous texture second to none.

Yield: 8 to 10 servings

3 pints double chocolate ice cream
2 tablespoons brandy
16 large macaroons, broken
¼ cup sherry

Set the ice cream in the refrigerator until it softens slightly. Add the brandy and mix in well. Sprinkle the sherry over the broken macaroons, then line a heavily greased melon-shaped mold with the broken macaroons. Spoon in the ice cream mix and freeze until firm, preferably overnight. Unmold to serve.

—Jean Powers
Hyde Park

The Ice Delivery Company caters to the home and originators of the (Ice When You Want It). Service in the ice industry. Main offices Race and Canal Streets. Call Canal 1772 or Valley 762.
—Choice Cookery, *circa 1900*

Eva Henry's Sweetpotato Pie

The secret to this classic dessert is the use of plenty of butter and canned milk.

Yield: 2 8-inch pies

4 pounds sweet potatoes
1 cup (2 sticks) butter
6 eggs
2 cups canned milk
Sugar to taste
1 teaspoon salt
2 teaspoons vanilla extract
2 teaspoons rum flavoring
1 teaspoon nutmeg
2 8-inch unbaked pie crusts

Cover the sweet potatoes with water and add a little salt. Boil in the jacket until fork tender. Preheat oven to 350 degrees F. While the sweet potatoes are hot, peel off the jackets and mash them in a bowl. Add the butter and beat well. Mix in the remaining ingredients and pour into the unbaked pie crust. Bake for 45 to 50 minutes.

Impossible Pie

Among Vinegar, Shoo-Fly Pie, and other pies that are created out of "wind pudding and air dip," this one has the ultimate benefit of making its own crust. These soft, moist crust bottoms on pies and pizzas are the latest rage for easy baking.

Yield: 2 8-inch pies

4 eggs
½ cup white or whole wheat flour
1 cup sugar
½ teaspoon baking powder
½ teaspoon salt

2 cups milk
4 tablespoons butter or margarine
1 teaspoon vanilla extract
7 ounces flaked coconut

Preheat oven to 350 degrees F. Place all of the ingredients in a blender and process for 30 seconds. Pour into two greased and floured 8-inch pie pans. Bake for 30 to 45 minutes, or until a knife inserted one inch from the side comes out clean.

—Mary Lou Wormus
St. Bernard

Fresh Strawberry Pie

At Aichholz Farm on Round Bottom Road, and other farms surrounding the city, U-PICK strawberries, peas, green beans, raspberries, corn, and tomatoes for economical eating or preserving. Some families bring a lunch and make it a pleasant, profitable outing.

Yield: 1 9-inch pie

1½ quarts strawberries, rinsed,
   hulled, and drained
¾ cup sugar
¼ cup water

1½ tablespoons cornstarch
2 tablespoons water
1 9-inch pie shell, baked
½ cup heavy cream, whipped

Purée or mash 1 cup of the strawberries. Place in a small saucepan with the sugar and ¼ cup water. Stir over medium heat until boiling. Mix the cornstarch with 2 tablespoons water. Stir the cornstarch mixture into the hot strawberries; boil 1 minute. Place the remaining strawberries in a large bowl and pour the cooked mixture over the berries. Toss gently, coating berries well. Spoon into pie shell. Chill until set, about 3 hours. Garnish with whipped cream.

—Aichholz Farm
Newtown

Cream Sherry Pie

This unique recipe is from the Meiers Wine Cellars collection and uses their award-winning No. 44 Cream Sherry.

Yield: 1 9-inch pie

1½ cups graham cracker crumbs	⅛ teaspoon salt
⅓ cup butter, melted	3 eggs, separated
½ cup cold water	½ cup cream sherry wine
1 envelope unflavored gelatin	1 cup heavy cream
⅔ cup sugar, divided	Red food coloring (optional)

Preheat oven to 350 degrees F. Combine the crumbs with the butter. Press in a 9-inch pie pan and bake for 10 minutes. Cool. While the crust is cooling, pour the water into a saucepan and sprinkle the gelatin over it. Add ⅓ cup of the sugar, salt, and egg yolks. Stir to blend. Place over a low heat and stir until the gelatin dissolves and the mixture thickens. Do not boil. Remove from heat and stir in the cream sherry. Chill until the mixture starts to mound slightly. Beat the egg whites until stiff, and then add the remaining sugar and beat until peaks are firm. Fold the meringue into the thickened mixture. Whip the cream; fold that into the mixture. Add food coloring if desired. Turn the mixture into the crust and chill several hours or overnight.

Hershey Bar Pie

From Beverly Garner's grandmother Augusta Gatch who claims it's so rich it makes your teeth ache.

Yield: 1 9-inch pie

20 marshmallows	½ pint heavy cream, whipped
½ cup milk	1 9-inch pie crust, baked
4 Hershey bars	

184

Combine the marshmallows, milk, and candy bars in the top of a double boiler. Cook over low heat until the ingredients are melted. Cool to room temperature. Fold in the whipped cream. Pour into the pie crust and refrigerate until the filling is set.

Note: A graham cracker crust may also be used.

Homemade Crisco Pie Crust Mix

Yield: about 8 cups mix

6 cups sifted flour   1 pound (2⅓ cups) Crisco
1 tablespoon salt

In a large mixing bowl mix the flour and salt. Cut in Crisco with a pastry blender or two knives until the mixture is uniform and very fine. Store in a covered container, such as an empty 3-pound Crisco can. No refrigeration is needed. To use, measure the mix into a bowl. Sprinkle water over the mix, a tablespoon at a time; toss lightly with a fork. When all water has been added, work dough into a firm ball.

For single-crust pie: Use 1½ cups of the mix and 3 tablespoons water.

For double-crust or lattice-top pie: Use 2¼ cups of mix and 4 tablespoons water.

—from a recent Crisco cookbook
Good Cooking Made Easy, 1978
Reprinted courtesy of
The Procter & Gamble Company

The History of Crisco

Crisco joined the Procter & Gamble line in 1911 as an absolutely new food product.

Long lists of suggested names were submitted by company people and by those who prepared Crisco advertising. The two leading choices, Krispo and Cryst, which some said were chosen to suggest the sound of hissing, frying fat, were eventually combined, and Crisco was the result. Crisco was first packed in 1½-pound cans and 50-pound wooden tubs, each displaying a light blue and white label, with the Crisco name printed inside the company's moon-and-stars trademark.

William Cooper Procter, then president of Procter & Gamble,

and his marketing staff decided on a dramatic marketing experiment to promote Crisco and to show homemakers how to get better results by using the brand in their cooking. Starting in 1913, six home economists traveled the country giving week-long demonstrations using Crisco in various cities. Under newspaper sponsorship and with advertisers of stoves, refrigerators, cooking utensils, flour, and spices cooperating, the events were announced as cooking schools. Following the demonstrations, souvenir baskets of various food samples, a 1½-pound can of Crisco, and a special Crisco cookbook were handed out to the eager audiences of homemakers who attended.

The earliest Crisco can had an eight-page circular cookbook cut to fit the lid. The first formal cookbook, printed in 1911 and entitled *Tested Crisco Recipes,* has been followed through the years by more than sixty Crisco cookbooks.

The brand also used radio to take its recipes to homemakers. The first three-station radio network programs the company ever used, back in 1923, consisted entirely of cake and cookie recipes read over the air for Crisco. Cooking experts from the *Ladies Home Journal* and other women's magazines created Crisco's early cookbooks and tested the recipes in their kitchens. Around 1923, however, Procter & Gamble set up its own test kitchen in Cincinnati for continuing tests and the creation of recipes.

When I Was a Boy

This poem is from "When I Was a Boy," a feature of the *Cincinnati Enquirer* since 1973; this episode ran Sunday, September 12, 1982.

When I was a boy,
I asked Grandma Hausman
to make me some kuechles,
a German deep-fried delicacy.
(My friend John Turek supplied
the spelling of kuechles,
which has an umlauted u.
Then he spelled umlaut.)
Grandma didn't answer me,
but she was "hard of hearing,"
so I asked her again, louder.
She still didn't hear me.
Mother said in a low voice,
"It seems to be she hears only
the things she wants to hear.
Ask her to play euchre."
Dad whispered, "That's not
a kind thing to say, Mary."
She said, "I can't hear you."
Grandma went out to the kitchen,
then called out, "C'mon, Jim,
I'll made the darned kuechles."
Mother looked at Dad.
Dad looked at the ceiling.
—Jim Hausman

Küchles

This word is probably derived from *kuchen* (cake) as "little cakes." Another possibility would be *kugel* (ball or globe). Although no one seemed certain about the exact spelling of this delicacy, all those German-descent households contacted knew of its existence and had "free-wheeling" recipes which ranged from doughnut to fritter batter. In some homes the kuchles or kugels were fried up especially for Halloween when the word referred to both the doughy balls and the bundled-up Halloween beggars themselves. They were received with joy and devoured immediately!

Yield: 2½ dozen balls

2 cups flour
¼ cup sugar
3 teaspoons baking powder
1 teaspoon salt
1 teaspoon nutmeg or mace
  (optional)

¼ cup vegetable oil
¾ cup milk
1 egg
Oil for frying
¼ cup sugar
1 teaspoon cinnamon

Sift together the flour, sugar, baking powder, salt, and spice. Add the oil, milk, and egg and stir with a fork until thoroughly mixed. Drop with a teaspoon (no bigger or they will not cook through) into hot oil and fry until golden brown. Drain. Stir together the remaining sugar and cinnamon and roll the warm cakes in the mixture.

Cookies and Candies

The George Washington—Chesapeake & Ohio Railway. Cincinnati Union Terminal is in the background. Drawing by Geneva South

189

Gingerbread

(Lebkuchen)

Ours is a homemade-cookie town. Baking cookies is probably the most common way Cincinnati mothers introduce their children to the world of cooking.

Yield: 6 dozen

½ cup honey
½ cup molasses
¾ cup sugar
1 egg
1 tablespoon lemon juice
1 teaspoon grated lemon rind
2½ cups flour

½ teaspoon baking soda
1 teaspoon cinnamon
1 teaspoon ground cloves
1 teaspoon allspice
1 teaspoon nutmeg
⅓ cup citron, cut up
⅓ cup chopped nuts

Glaze

1 cup sugar
½ cup water

¼ cup confectioners' sugar

Mix the honey and molasses in a small pan. Bring to a boil. Stir in the sugar, egg, lemon juice, and rind. Sift the flour and then sift the dry ingredients together. Blend the dry ingredients with the honey mixture. Mix in the citron and nuts. Chill the dough overnight. When ready to make the cookies, heat the oven to 400 degrees F. Roll out a small amount of the dough at a time, keeping the rest chilled. Roll dough ¼-inch thick on a lightly floured board. Cut in 2½-by-1½-inch oblongs. Place 1 inch apart on a greased baking sheet. Bake 10 to 12 minutes or until no imprints remain when touched lightly.

While the cookies are baking, put together the glaze. Blend the sugar and water in a small saucepan. Boil it until it threads. Remove from the heat. Stir in the confectioners' sugar. Brush the glaze over the cookies immediately after they are removed from the oven. Cool and store in an airtight container with cut orange or apple pieces for a few days to mellow.

Note: If the glaze becomes sugary while using, reheat it slightly, adding a little water.

—International Girl Scout Potluck
Finneytown, 1968

Sandwich Cookies

From the donor's vast collection of cookie recipes, these seem to be people's favorites.

Yield: about 7 dozen

1½ cups (3 sticks) butter
1¼ cup sugar
1 egg
3½ cups flour

Red raspberry jelly, currant jelly, or
   rose hip jelly
Confectioners' sugar as needed

Preheat oven to 350 degrees F. Cream the butter; add sugar and egg. Add flour and mix well. Knead. Roll between sheets of floured wax paper until very thin. Cut out small rounds. Bake for about ten minutes. Form sandwiches by putting two rounds together with jelly in between. Dip in confectioners' sugar.

Note: If you are very ambitious, you can ice every round before you put the sandwiches together and decorate with colored sugar or ground nuts.

—Ingrid Nutzel
Anderson Township

Cinnamon Sticks

Yield: about 7 dozen

3 egg whites
10 ounces confectioners' sugar
1½ teaspoons cinnamon

Grated rind of 1 small lemon
6 ounces ground almonds
4 ounces ground pecans

Preheat oven to 350 degrees F. Beat the egg whites until stiff and add the sugar, cinnamon, and lemon rind. Set aside ⅓ of this mixture. Add the ground nuts to the remaining mixture. Roll out; since the dough is soft, this is easiest done between sheets of floured waxed paper. Cut into strips. Ice with the remaining egg white mixture. Place on greased sheets. Bake for 15 to 20 minutes.

—Ingrid Nutzel

Log House Cookies

This quaint cookie and cutter were designed by the members of the Anderson Township Historical Society in honor of the Miller-Leuser Pioneer Log House built on Clough Road in 1796.

Yield: about 4 dozen

1 cup sugar
½ cup (1 stick) butter, at room
   temperature
1 egg
2½ tablespoons sour milk
¾ teaspoon vanilla extract
¾ teaspoon salt

2¼ cups flour
½ teaspoon baking soda
1 teaspoon cream of tartar
1 tablespoon cold water
1 tablespoon molasses or sorghum
Sugar for dusting

Preheat oven to 375 degrees F. Cream the sugar and butter. Beat in the egg, milk, vanilla, and salt. Sift together the flour, soda, and cream of tartar; mix with the butter mixture. Blend into a fairly stiff dough. Roll out to about ¼-inch on a floured board with a floured rolling pin. Cut into log houses and carefully place on a greased cookie tin. In a small cup, mix the cold water and molasses. Brush each cookie lightly with this mixture, and then sprinkle with sugar. Bake for about ten minutes or until lightly browned.

Note: These cookies may be iced to outline the chimney, door, and some logs of the house.

—Marjorie A. Frame
Anderson Township

Peanut Bars

Tales of these melt-in-the-mouth confections are widespread in the hills of eastern Cincinnati. They are sold at Ripley church socials and reportedly sell out as fast as they are brought in by the bakers.

Yield: about 3 dozen

Cake

4 eggs
2 cups sugar
2 cups cake flour
2 teaspoons baking powder

½ teaspoon salt
½ teaspoon vanilla extract
1 cup milk, scalded

Icing

1 pound confectioners' sugar
½ cup (1 stick) butter
1 teaspoon vanilla extract
½ teaspoon salt

Milk as needed
1 pound white salted peanuts,
  ground

Preheat oven to 350 degrees F. Line an ungreased 13-by-16-inch pan with waxed paper. In a deep, narrow bowl beat the eggs and sugar until light and fluffy, and then beat ten minutes more. Mix the flour, baking powder, and salt in another bowl and gradually fold into the egg mixture. Add the vanilla and the barely hot milk and blend well. Pour into the pan and bake for 35 minutes. To make the icing, mix the confectioners' sugar, butter, vanilla, and salt with enough milk to make the icing thin. When the cake is cool, cut into oblong pieces. Dip each piece into the icing and roll in the ground peanuts. Place on waxed paper until firm.

—Arvella Hefferman
Ripley Riverview Garden Club Cookbook, 1976

Honey Spice Cookie

(Melomakarona)

Every July the Greek Festival is held at Holy Trinity Greek Orthodox Church in Finneytown. There is music, dancing, and an extravagant Greek menu including *dolmathes, pastitsio, gyro* sandwiches with delectable cucumber sauce, *loukomateh*—a freshly fried hot honey puff—*baklava*, and this popular cookie, all to be sampled with a glass or two of Greek wine.

Yield: about 7 dozen

1 cup (2 sticks) butter or margarine
1 cup salad oil
½ cup sugar
Rind from 1 orange, grated
2 teaspoons cinnamon
1½ teaspoons ground cloves
¼ teaspoon nutmeg

6 to 7 cups sifted flour
1 teaspoon baking powder
½ cup orange juice
½ teaspoon baking soda
1 cup (or more) warmed honey with
  a little water added.

Preheat oven to 325 degrees F. Melt the butter and then cool slightly. Place the butter and oil into a bowl and beat with a mixer until creamy. Add the sugar and continue beating. Place the orange rind in a cup, add all

193

of the spices, and mix with a fork. Place this mixture into the butter mixture and continue beating. Sift the flour and baking powder together and begin adding it to the butter mixture, a little at a time. When it becomes too difficult for the mixer, beat by hand until half of the flour is beaten in. Place the orange juice in a full cup measure and add the baking soda (it will foam). Add this to the flour mixture and continue beating, adding the rest of the flour until the dough is thick, smooth, and soft enough to hold shape. Pat it out to ½-inch thicknesses on a table. Cut out circles with a glass, and then cut circles in half with a knife to form half-moon shapes. Place on an ungreased baking sheet and bake for 30 to 35 minutes or until golden brown. Cool completely, then dip each one in the honey and water mixture, and place on waxed paper to dry.

—Angie Sampson
Holy Trinity Greek Orthodox Church

Scotch Shortbread

Yield: 5 dozen

1½ cups (3 sticks) butter, at room
  temperature

1 cup sugar
3½ cups flour

Preheat oven to 300 degrees F. Cream the butter and sugar together. Gradually sift in the flour. Mix with an electric beater until it is too stiff to beat. Knead with the hands for about 5 minutes. Spread out and press into an ungreased 13-by-9-inch cookie sheet. Pierce all over with a fork. Bake for at least an hour. Remove and cut into pieces.

Note: The shortbread will not turn brown unless you are burning it. The bottom will turn a light brown but the top will appear creamy in color.

—Mary Ann Will

Spice or Pepper Cookie

(Pfeffernusse)

Yield: 5 to 6 dozen

½ cup (1 stick) butter, at room
  temperature
⅔ cup dark brown sugar
1 egg
3 cups sifted flour

1 teaspoon ginger
1 teaspoon ground cloves
¼ teaspoon pepper
¼ teaspoon salt
Confectioners' sugar for coating

194

Preheat oven to 325 degrees F. Combine the ingredients, except for the confectioners' sugar, in the order given. Knead until the dough no longer clings to your hands. Form cookies about the size and shape of pecans. Bake on a greased cookie sheet for about 15 minutes. Cool, and then roll in confectioners' sugar. Store airtight.

—International Girl Scout Potluck, 1968
Finneytown

Butterscotch Brownies

Yield: 2 dozen

½ cup (1 stick) unsalted butter
2 cups packed brown sugar
2 eggs
1 teaspoon vanilla extract
1¼ cups flour

½ teaspoon baking powder
½ teaspoon salt
1 cup chopped pecans
½ cup chopped milk chocolate

Preheat oven to 350 degrees F. Melt the butter and stir in the brown sugar. Cook and stir until the mixture is hot and bubbly. Cool 10 minutes. Beat in the eggs and the vanilla. Stir in the flour, baking powder, and salt. Fold in the pecans and chocolate. Bake in a greased 9-by-13-inch pan for 25 to 30 minutes. Cool and cut into bars.

—Lauretta Omeltschenko
Western Hills

Springerle

You'll need a springerle (pronounced springer-la) board or rolling pin to make these cookies. Traditionally they are dried until hard, and then placed in a bowl with cold or warm milk to be broken up and eaten.

Yield: 2 to 3 dozen

2 eggs
1 cup sugar
2¼ cups flour
½ teaspoon baking powder

Dash salt
Scant ¼ teaspoon anise oil or
    ½ teaspoon crushed anise seed

Beat the eggs and sugar together thoroughly. Sift together the flour, baking powder, and salt. Stir the flour into the egg mixture until the dough is well blended and very stiff. Add the anise oil or seeds and beat again. Refrigerate the dough for 3 to 4 hours. Roll the dough out about ⅓-inch on a lightly floured board, into an oblong the size of the springerle board or roller. Press the well-floured board or roller firmly down onto the dough to emboss the designs. Cut out little squares; dry on a lightly floured board for at least 10 hours at room temperature. Preheat the oven to 325 degrees F. Bake the cookies 12 to 15 minutes on a lightly greased baking sheet. The cookies should mellow 3 or 4 days before using.

—International Girl Scouts Potluck
Finneytown, 1968

Jelly Bars

You could make these delectable cookies with any preserve, but why not the best? Clearbrook Farms Preserves of Fairfax were created by owners Jerome Cohen and Stanley Liscow who were tired of remaining anonymous. For over fifty years they made the jellies we ate in jelly donuts, jelly rolls, and other bakery sweets, but their special preserves were shared only with relatives, colleagues, and friends. In 1977 all that changed, and the Cincinnati delicacy is now sold in specialty food shops nationwide.

Yield: about 3 dozen bars

1 cup butter (2 sticks), at room
  temperature
1 cup sugar
1 egg

1 teaspoon vanilla extract
2½ cups flour
Preserves as needed

Cream the butter and sugar. Add the egg and vanilla and beat until well blended. Blend in the flour. Remove about a cup of the batter after it is mixed and place it in the freezer. Pat the remaining dough evenly in an ungreased 11-by-15-inch jelly roll pan. This takes some work and will result in a thin layer. Spread any choice of preserves over the top. After the cup of batter in the freezer has hardened, shred the dough over the top of the jelly bars as a topping. Use a grater or food processor. Bake at 350 degrees F. for 20 to 25 minutes. Cool and cut into bars.

—Party Planners Catering Company

German Sour Cream Twists

These sweet morsels have been a conversation stopper at many a *kaffee klatsch*, that is, coffee with "gossip." They are equally appreciated boxed and given as a gift to a special friend.

Yield: about 5 dozen

3½ cups sifted flour
1 teaspoon salt
½ cup shortening
½ cup butter
1 package dry yeast
¼ cup warm water

¾ cup sour cream
1 whole egg and 2 egg yolks, well beaten
1 teaspoon vanilla extract
1 cup sugar

Sift the flour and salt into a mixing bowl. Blend the shortening and butter together and cut in the flour mixture. Dissolve the yeast in water; stir it into the flour mixture. Add the sour cream, eggs, and vanilla. Mix well with the hands. Cover with a damp cloth and refrigerate two hours. Roll half of the dough on a sugared board into an oblong 8-by-16 inches. Fold the ends toward the center, ends overlapping (into thirds). Sprinkle with sugar; roll again to same size. Add more sugar and repeat. Roll about ¼-inch thick. Cut into strips about 1-by-4 inches. Twist ends in opposite directions, stretching the dough slightly. Bend in the shape of a horseshoe on an ungreased baking sheet, pressing the ends to keep shape. Repeat this process with the other half of the dough. Bake at 375 degrees F. about 15 minutes or until delicately brown. Take from baking sheet immediately.

Note: The twists may be iced while still warm with a mixture of confectioners' sugar, milk, and almond flavoring.

—Kathryn Pendell
Mt. Carmel

Jam Center Cookies

Yield: about 2½ dozen cookies

½ cup butter, at room temperature
1 teaspoon vanilla extract
½ cup brown sugar, packed

1½ cups flour, sifted
2 tablespoons milk
Preserves as needed

Preheat oven to 375 degrees F. Mix the butter, vanilla, and brown sugar until light and fluffy. Blend in the flour and milk. Shape into 1-inch balls and place on an ungreased cookie sheet. Bake about 5 minutes. Pull out of the oven and using the back of a small measuring spoon, make a depression. Fill with your choice of preserves, jams, marmalades, or jellies. Return to the oven and bake another 5 to 7 minutes or until lightly browned. Cool before eating.

—Party Planners Catering Company

The Island Queen. Steamboats were important to the early success of Ohio Grove, later called Coney Island. The first Island Queen, a sidewheel excursion boat, served the Coney Island Company from 1869 until it burned at the Cincinnati wharf in 1922. Shuttling back and forth from the Public Landing to the park—its calliope piping merrily—this second Island Queen had five decks and could accommodate 4,000 passengers. It delighted its passengers until tragedy struck in September, 1947 when it exploded and burned in Pittsburgh. Television personality Ruth Lyons was among those crowd pleasers who entertained on some of those never-to-be-forgotten moonlit rides. Drawing by Tom Ward

Candy's Cream Cheese Brownies

This recipe is from a cookbook Candy Newman was working on, shared with us by her loving father Herman Andrew Newman. It is a joy to print the labors of this generous girl, so beloved by her mother, television star Ruth Lyons, a small tribute to their exemplary family life.

Yield: 16 brownies

1 4-ounce package German sweet chocolate
5 tablespoons butter or margarine
1 3-ounce package cream cheese, at room temperature
1 cup sugar

3 eggs
½ cup plus one tablespoon flour
2 teaspoons vanilla extract
½ teaspoon baking powder
¼ teaspoon salt
½ cup chopped pecans

Preheat oven to 350 degrees F. Melt the chocolate and butter over a very low heat. Stir until well blended. Cool. Cream the cheese. Gradually add the sugar. Cream until fluffy. Blend in the eggs, flour, and vanilla. Add the baking powder and salt. Blend in the chocolate mixture. Mix well until thoroughly blended. Last of all blend in the pecans. Spread in a greased 8 or 9-inch square pan. Bake for 35 to 40 minutes. Cool. Cut into squares.

Chocolate Drop Cookies

(Schokoladeplatzchen)

Yield: about 3 dozen

¾ cups finely ground unblanched almonds
1 11-ounce bar German Sweet Chocolate, grated fine

3 egg whites
½ cup sugar
⅛ teaspoon salt

Preheat oven to 275 degrees F. Mix the nuts and chocolate together and set aside. Beat the egg whites until very stiff peaks form, and then gradually add the sugar and salt. Beat an additional two minutes. Fold in the chocolate and nuts. Drop by teaspoonsful on a well-greased baking sheet. Bake for 35 to 40 minutes.

—Helen Schwiegeraht

Vanillekipfel

Mürber Teig*
Mehl 35 dkg
Butter 21 dkg
Vanillezucker 11 dkg

Mandeln 11 dkg
Dotter 2
Vanillezucker 12 dkg

Mehl, Butter, Zucker, geschälte, geriebene Mandeln und Dotter werden auf dem Brett zu einem Teig verarbeitet. Daraus formt man kleine Kipfel, die auf einem Blech lichtgebacken und noch heiss in Vanillezucker gedreht werden.

*Mürbe Teige sind auf dem Brett zu verarbeiten und bedürfen einem halbstündigen Rast im Kühlen.

—Nicole Steindler
College Hill

Vanilla Crescent Cookies

Yield: about 7 dozen

2⅓ cups flour
1 cup (2 sticks) butter, at room
  temperature
¾ cup vanilla sugar (see Note)

1 cup finely ground blanched
  almonds
2 egg yolks
Vanilla sugar for cooking

Work the flour, butter, vanilla sugar, almonds, and egg yolks into a dough. Shape into two balls and refrigerate for one half hour. Preheat oven to 350 degrees F. Cut off small pieces of dough and shape them into crescents the thickness of your little finger, about two inches long. Place on an ungreased cookie sheet and bake about 10 minutes, or until light brown. Roll hot crescents in vanilla sugar.

Note: Prepare vanilla sugar by placing a vanilla bean or two into a tightly covered jar with confectioners' sugar. Keep the jar closed for several weeks.

200

Lemon Crackers

One pint of lard, 2½ cups granulated sugar, whites of two eggs, 1 pint of sweet milk, 1 tablespoon baker's ammonia, 1 tablespoon lemon oil, 1 teaspoon of salt. Beat eggs until they froth. Put the ammonia in milk. Add flour to make it all as stiff as can be mixed. Roll as thin as possible, cut in squares and bake in a quick oven.

Note: You can buy lemon oil at a drug store, baker's ammonia at old-fashioned shops.

—Bessie Miller
Christian Women's Missionary Cook Book, 1921

Black Walnut Macaroons

Cincinnati's climate is favorable for the exotic black walnut tree which still grows in abundance outside the city proper.

2 yolks of eggs	1 teaspoon cinnamon
1 whole egg	1 teaspoon baking powder
2 tablespoons molasses	½ teaspoon baking soda (dissolved
2¼ cups sifted flour	in a little water)
1½ cups light brown sugar	1 cup broken walnut meats
½ cup butter, melted	

Mix all the ingredients, adding the walnuts last. It makes a very stiff batter. Drop from a spoon onto a buttered pan and bake in a quick oven.

—Louise Hahn
Tested Recipes, 1916

Buckeyes

Ohio is known as the Buckeye State, and these candies are made to resemble the buckeye seed. The real buckeye is reputedly poisonous.

Yield: 3 to 4 dozen

½ cup (1 stick) butter or margarine, at room temperature
1 1-pound box confectioners' sugar
1½ cups peanut butter
1 teaspoon vanilla extract
1 12-ounce package real chocolate chips
¼ stick paraffin

Cream the butter, confectioners' sugar, peanut butter, and vanilla. Form into small balls and refrigerate overnight. Melt the chocolate chips and paraffin in the top of a double boiler. Stick a toothpick in the candy ball and dip it into the chocolate mixture. Leave part of the ball uncovered so that it resembles a buckeye, but cover the toothpick hole. Place on waxed paper to cool and harden. These candies can be frozen.

—Phyllis Martin
Anderson Township

Mints

1 8-ounce package cream cheese
2 pounds confectioners' sugar
Food colorings: yellow, pink, green
Lemon flavoring to taste
Mint flavoring to taste
Wintergreen flavoring to taste

Knead the cream cheese and confectioners' sugar together with the hands until smooth. Divide into three parts and add the colorings and flavorings: yellow for lemon; pink for mint; green for wintergreen. Mix well. Shape as desired. Refrigerate.

—Bev Nye
A Family Raised on Sunshine, 1977

Potato Candy

Some called them Cinnamon Potatoes, Irish Potatoes or Murphies, but they were the rage amongst everyone in the 1940s.

2–3 red potatoes, medium size
dash salt
1 can (4 ounces) coconut
1 teaspoon vanilla extract
2–3 boxes confectioners' sugar
cinnamon for rolling

Boil potatoes; drain and mash as for regular mashed potatoes. (You should end up with about one cup of mashed potatoes.) Add salt, coconut, and vanilla while potatoes are still hot. Gradually add the confectioners' sugar as needed, this fondant should be thick enough to knead like bread. Knead thoroughly until very stiff. Break off small amounts and form into miniature Idaho potatoes, placing them on wax paper. They will harden in a few minutes. When finished, place each potato in a small amount of cinnamon and turn to coat evenly.

—Mrs. Clyde Crawford
Covington

Almonds and Brandy

This agreeable remedy for "Weakness and Anemia in Women" comes from a book definitively titled *A Book of Recipes Covering Three Generations of the Farny and Wurlitzer Family (1791–1925)*. It was compiled for the family by Leonie Farny Wurlitzer and Marguerite Farny Strobel. It is exquisitely printed, is bound in black leather, and has edges stamped in gold. The Farnys came to Cincinnati from Alsace, France. Paintings by Henry Farny, brother of the two women, hang in the Cincinnati Art museum.

Put one cup of sugar into a pan with a little water. Let it boil until it draws a thread. Add 1 flat teaspoon cinnamon and while the sugar is boiling roast the shelled almonds with the brown skin left on, lightly in the oven. When the sugar is ready pour the almonds in, stirring them briskly with a wooden spoon until the sugar has coated the almonds. Take and spread them on a platter and break them apart and put them into a jar. Then take every night five or six of these almonds before going to bed. Eat them and drink a tablespoon of good old French brandy. Do that every night for a month and if you feel benefitted keep on several months until you feel well and strong. But to get good results it must be taken every day.

—*Janet W. Stites,*
granddaughter of
Leonie Farny Wurlitzer

Rock Candy

Back to the days of the penny candy store, which oftentimes was only a glass-covered counter in a drug store or general store. With that valuable copper cent you could choose from red and black licorice strands, bullseyes, Tootsie-pops, chocolate covered mint patties, nut bars, peanut butter cups, fruit slices, or perhaps a chunk of crystallized rock candy on a string.

Yield: It's up to you

4 cups water	8 cups sugar

Bring the water to a boil. Pour in the sugar and stir until it is completely dissolved. Into a measuring cup pour about ¼ cup of the sugar water. Cover the cup with foil. Pour the rest of the sugar water into a quart canning jar and put on the lid. Two days later the water in the measuring cup will have evaporated and you will have some crystals. Tie a 6-inch string around one crystal. Cut a cardboard circle to fit inside the quart jar lid. Punch a hole in the circle and push the string through the hole, tying a knot. Heat the sugar water and remaining crystals in a pot until the crystals have dissolved. Pour the liquid back into the jar. Cool about 20 minutes. Put the cardboard circle on the jar so the tiny crystal dangles in the sugar water, and screw on the lid. One week later, a small chunk of rock candy will have appeared at the end of the string. Leave it in for a larger chunk.

—Barbara Bruce
Mt. Washington

Sauces and Pickles

Mexican Taco Season Mix

Cincinnati homemaker Beverly Nye, author of three domestic books, has her own national cable TV show, "At Home with Beverly Nye." She also appears weekly on the local Bob Braun Show. Her recipes are popular because they are simple, economical, and delicious.

¼ cup dried minced onion flakes
4 teaspoons cornstarch
3 tablespoons salt
4 tablespoons chili powder
3 teaspoons cumin

1½ teaspoons oregano
3 teaspoons dried minced garlic
3 teaspoons hot crushed red
   pepper
2 teaspoons beef bouillon

Mix all the ingredients together and store in a tight container. Two tablespoons equals one commercial package.

—*A Family Raised on Rainbows*, 1979

Lemon Catchup

Cut nine large lemons into thin slices, and take out the seeds. Prepare, by pounding them in a mortar, 2 ounces of mustard seed, half an ounce of black pepper, half an ounce of nutmeg, a quarter of an ounce of mace, and a quarter of an ounce of cloves. Slice thin two ounces of horseradish. Strew over them 3 ounces of fine salt. Add a quart of the best vinegar. Boil the whole 20 minutes. Then put it warm into a jar and let it stand three weeks closely covered. Stir it up daily. Then strain it through a sieve, and put it up in small bottles to flavor fish and other sauces. This is sometimes called Lemon Pickle.

—White's New Cook-Book, *a small booklet*
"Embracing Temperate and Economical Receipts
for Domestic Liquors and Cookery" by
Daniel T. White, 1840

Chili Sauce

Yield: 3½ pints

12 tomatoes
4 onions
2 green peppers
1 cup vinegar

2 cups sugar
2 tablespoons salt
2 tablespoons mixed spices tied in a
    cloth bag

Peel and cut vegetables real small. Cook four hours on low heat. Stir when it begins to thicken so it doesn't stick or burn. Seal in hot jars.

—*A Book of Favorite Recipes*, 1981

Chili Sauce

Three hot peppers, chopped fine, seeds out; 1 peck of ripe tomatoes, 2 onions, 2 cups of sugar, 2 tablespoons salt, 1 tablespoon each of cloves, allspice, nutmeg and ginger and 1 quart of good vinegar. Cook 2½ hours. Put in bottles or quart jars.

—Christian Women's Missionary Society Cookbook, 1921

Rose Butter

Take a glass jar, put on the bottom a layer of butter, and each day put in rose leaves, adding layers of butter, and when full, cover tight, and use the butter for articles to be flavored with rose water.

—Miss Beecher's Domestic Receipt-Book, 1868

Horseradish

Cut one horseradish root (about ¾ pound) into as few pieces as possible so as to protect your eyes from the fierce aroma. Place these pieces in a blender and do not look down into the blender after grinding. Process well. Add a little salt, then transfer the ground horseradish to a narrow bottle. Add enough vinegar to cover. Let it stand at least overnight before using.

—Fradie Kramer

207

*Eighth and Plum. St. Peter in Chains Cathedral, called lovingly by its people "White Angel,"
was dedicated on November 2, 1845 and re-dedicated in 1957. City Hall was dedicated in 1893
and became a National Landmark in 1972. Drawing by Geneva South*

German Mustard

This is a modern version of an old recipe that was complicated and time-consuming.

Yield: about 1 cup

¾ cup apple cider vinegar, divided
½ cup hot water
5 tablespoons dry mustard
¼ cup mustard seeds
¼ cup chopped onion
2 teaspoons brown molasses or honey

2 garlic cloves, crushed
½ teaspoon tarragon
¼ teaspoon dill seeds
¼ teaspoon cinnamon
¼ teaspoon allspice
Salt and pepper to taste

Place one-fourth cup of the vinegar, the hot water, dry mustard, and mustard seeds in the blender and process until the seeds are split or ground to personal preference. (The finer the grind, the smoother the mustard; most prefer a coarser blend.) Let the mixture sit for two hours at room temperature. Combine the remaining vinegar and all the other ingredients in a saucepan. Bring to a boil, boil for one minute, and let stand until the mustard mixture is ready. Then strain this liquid into the blender, pressing the spices against the sides of the strainer to extract all the flavor. Stir, and then process until the mixture is the consistency of a coarse purée. Transfer this mixture into the top half of a simmering double boiler and cook, stirring frequently, fifteen or twenty minutes until thickened. The mustard will thicken more as it cools. Pour into a jar and cover lightly until cooled. Store in the refrigerator.

Note: Multiplying this recipe by four will result in approximately six ½-pint jars of mustard to give as holiday gifts.

Mustard Pickles

Is there any visitor to Findlay Market who can resist the tempting morsels of the Pickle Stand? Sweet pickles, sour pickles, black olives, green olives, corn relish, pig's feet, peppers, watermelon pickles, stuffed mangoes, mustards, and this most popular item, which will send any salivary gland into a frenzy.

---

1 quart small whole cucumbers
1 quart large sliced cucumbers
1 quart green tomatoes, sliced
1 quart small button onions

1 large cauliflower divided into
  flowerettes
4 green peppers cut fine

Make a brine of 4 quarts of water and 1 pint of salt, pour it over the mixture of vegetables and let soak 24 hours. Heat just enough to scald it and turn into a colander to drain. Mix one cup flour, 6 tablespoons ground mustard, 1 tablespoon turmeric with enough cold vinegar to make a smooth paste. Add 1½ cups sugar, ½ cup celery seeds, 2 tablespoons white mustard seeds and enough vinegar to make 2 quarts in all. Boil this mixture until it thickens and is smooth, stirring all the time, then add the vegetables and cook until well heated through. Put in Mason jars.
—The House-keeper's Guide and Everybody's Cook-Book, 1864

Pickled Pig's Feet

This is a very old recipe imported from Brown County. When a hog was butchered every edible portion was savoured, and still is.

Yield: 1 quart

4 pig's feet   Salt as needed

Pickling Syrup

1 pint vinegar
1 pint water
1 teaspoon celery seed
1 tablespoon mustard seed
4 tablespoons horseradish
½ cup sugar

1 onion, chopped
1½ teaspoons salt
4 whole cloves
½ cinnamon stick
1 red pepper pod (optional)

Scald the feet and scrub them well. Put them into a pan, cover with cold water, and bring to a boil. Add one tablespoon salt for each quart of water. Cover and simmer until tender, about three hours. While the feet are simmering make the pickling syrup. Put all of the ingredients into a pan and bring to a boil. Boil a few minutes and then turn off the fire. When the pig's feet are tender, place them into the syrup, and set aside for two hours. Then bring to a boil for five minutes and pack into sterilized jars. Remove the cinnamon stick. Seal.

—Mary Rose Pitzer
Mt. Washington

Pickled Walnuts

Take a hundred nuts, an ounce of cloves, an ounce of allspice, an ounce of nutmeg, an ounce of whole pepper, an ounce of race ginger, an ounce of horseradish, half pint of mustard seed, tied in a bag, and four cloves of garlic.

Wipe the nuts, prick with a pin, and put them in a pot, sprinkling the spice as you lay them in; then add two tablespoons of salt; boil sufficient vinegar to fill the pot, and pour it over the nuts and spices. Cover the jar close, and keep it for a year, when the pickles will be ready for use.

The vinegar makes an excellent catsup.

—Miss Beecher's Domestic Receipt-Book, 1868

Beer Marinade

This marinade will flavor and tenderize a pot roast, and can be added to the gravy liquid if desired.

3 tablespoons sugar	1 12-ounce bottle beer
1 tablespoon salt	½ cup salad oil
1 teaspoon whole cloves	Juice of 1 large onion
2 ice cubes	Dash pepper
Grated rind of 1 large lemon	

Mix the dry ingredients. Add the ice cubes, lemon rind, and enough beer to make a smooth paste. Add the salad oil slowly, stirring rapidly. Add the remaining beer and the rest of the ingredients and pour mixture into a pint jar. Store in the refrigerator and shake vigorously before using.

—The Hudepohl Brewing Company

Herb Vinegars

Rosella began growing and working with herbs in 1939 when her family moved to twenty acres in Silverton to bring up their children in the "country." The herbs planted on a quarter acre were so prolific that the pastime became a profitable business. She is currently working on the third edition of the *Guide*.

"You will be surprised at how people, especially those who have never used herbs, welcome bottles of vinegar. Save attractive pint and half pint bottles with screw tops (or use corks) for herb vinegar to be used as gifts.

"The directions are easy. Cut the leafy tips just before blooming for the most flavor. Wash quickly and shake off the water. Bruise between palms or with a potato masher and fill loosely a wide-mouthed jar. If seeds are used, these are bruised before infusing. A two-quart pickle jar is convenient. Pour the vinegar over and let stand in a warm place for two to three weeks. After two weeks, smell and taste the vinegar to see if it seems strong enough. If not, leave for another few days. When ready, strain through a piece of muslin or a coffee filter and bottle."

Recipes

To two quarts add five parts purple basil, 1 part thyme, 1 part marjoram, 6 cloves garlic, sliced.

To two quarts vinegar add two parts tarragon, 1 part fennel seed, 1 part chervil, 1 part thyme, 1 part burnet, and garlic. (This is good with fish.)

To two quarts vinegar add 1 part basil, 1 part lemon thyme, 1 part rosemary, 1 part crushed celery seed, and the peel of 1 lemon with pith removed.

Add orange peels to cider vinegar. While not an herbal vinegar it is too good to leave out.

—Rosella F. Mathieu
The Herb Grower's Complete Guide, 1954

Hamersville, Ohio
September 7, 1938

Dear Mary,

Received your letter yesterday and intended to get this in this morning's mail but I failed. Have been picking beans and getting them ready to cold pack. When I get them shelled I'll have 18 quarts. Some job for one but they're the Pitzer Beans and well worth the trouble. I canned corn Monday and will can more Friday. Then I think I'll be almost done canning for I have nearly all my cans filled now.

Sure glad you liked your mango pickles, we always liked them fixed that way. Yes, Mary, you can leave your cucumber pickles in a stone jar. They'll be just as good as in glass cans. Keep a cloth tied over them after you get them done for sometimes the gnats bother them.

Dad told Richard it would be a lot of trouble to make pickles with that recipe you sent but I guess men don't realize how much work it does take to fix good things to eat. But I don't mind the work if things are really good after they are done.

Richard sure had a nice time while at your house. He has been quite busy since he came home from the city. He started to school yesterday.

Ora and Gerald are putting in tobacco today. I think they can finish tomorrow if nothing happens. It rained a real nice shower here a few minutes ago. We needed it badly too.

I am going to paint and paper my living room next week. Let me know about your pickles and come up when you can.

With love,
from Cora

Homemade Sauerkraut

Yield: 1 large crock sauerkraut

1 bushel green cabbage
Salt as needed

Proportion: 10 pounds of cabbage
to ½ cup salt

Quarter the cabbages and shred them with a kraut cutter or in a food processor. Put a thick layer of cut cabbage in the crock, and then cover it with salt. Repeat until all the cabbages are used, ladling off excess

213

water. To keep gnats out, cover the opening of the crock with a cloth and tie it down with a string. Then cover with a heavy plate or clean hardwood board and place a large rock or weight on the cover. (Do not use limestone.) Check occasionally. As the kraut cures, remove the topmost fermented layer and drain off any excess liquid. The kraut will cure in one to three weeks depending on the temperature at which it is stored. This sauerkraut will keep in a cold place until it's all eaten up. However, you can process it if you prefer.

—The Lauderbach family
Russellville

Mango Pickle

(Stuffed Green Peppers)

I soak them overnight in salt water. Next morning grind the cabbage and season to taste with salt and pepper. Stuff the mangoes with cabbage. The amount of syrup or vinegar to use will depend on the amount of mangoes you have. I use 1 cup of sugar and 1 pint of vinegar unless the vinegar is very strong and then use more sugar. You may use spices if you like but all I use is mustard seed. Bring the sugar and vinegar to a boil then carefully drop the stuffed mangoes into the vinegar mix. Leave them in the syrup for about ten minutes, then place in jars, cover with the syrup and seal.

—Cora Brooks Pitzer, age 87
Hamersville

To Pickle Mushrooms

Stew them in salted water, just enough to keep them from sticking. When tender, pour off the water, and pour on hot spiced vinegar. Then cork them tight if you wish to keep them long. Poison ones will turn black if an onion is stewed with them, and then all must be thrown away.

—Miss Beecher's Domestic Receipt Book, 1868

New Year's Eve

Among the many local superstitions surrounding the beginning of the New Year is the solemn eating of various foodstuffs precisely at midnight. Herring and sauerkraut are most common lucky favorites. Simultaneously, you must kiss your beloved to ensure love throughout the year and make a considerable noise at the front door to ward off evil spirits. All this within the twelve alloted chimes!

To ensure good fortune it is advised that you place a dime on the windowsill before midnight. If, on the following morning, the dime has disappeared, financial gain will be yours. If the dime is still there, woe to your pocketbook.

Mary Agnes O'Fury Hart brought with her from Ireland this questionable recommendation: Never let a lady enter your home until a man has come in first. A man brings in the New Year.

A champagne toast is also in order, along with drinks and snacks throughout the evening.

Pickled Green Tomatoes

When Therese and her three sisters were married in the 1930s their mother gave each of them a "Ball Book" of canning instructions. Each one canned green tomatoes using the Ball Book as a guide and perfected her own recipe.

Yield: about 4 quarts

1 gallon green tomatoes	1 tablespoon celery seed
6 onions	1 tablespoon whole allspice
½ cup salt	1 garlic clove
2 pods pepper	1½ cups sugar or brown sugar
1 tablespoon mustard seed	4 cups vinegar

Slice the tomatoes and onions ¼-inch thick. Place in a bowl in layers, sprinkling salt on each layer. Let stand overnight, and then drain well. Tie the seasonings in a cloth bag. Boil the sugar, seasonings, and vinegar 10 minutes. Cool slightly. Add the tomatoes and onions and simmer for 30 minutes. Pack in hot Ball jars and seal at once.

—Therese Hart (Aunt Dee-dee)

Herb Butter

Make a year's supply of herb butter in July or early August. If stored in the deep freeze, the herbs in the butter will retain their green color and flavor for a year or longer. The following herbs can be used as a blend: tarragon, dill, parsley, chives, thyme, chervil, sweet marjoram, summer savory, and cress. As few as three herbs may be used but eight or nine make a delicious blend. Cream the butter (unsalted butter is preferred.) Cut the chives into small bits with scissors. Chop with leaves (no stems) in a wooden bowl with a handchopper. *Do not use a food chopper.* For one pound of butter use two tablespoons chopped herbs. For ten pounds use 1½ cups chopped herbs.

—Daisy Sticksel
Newtown

216

Tutti-Fruitti

Take a large glass jar with lid; ½ cup of brandy to start conserve. Now begin
with early fruit, strawberries, etc. by taking one cup of fruit, 1 cup of sugar
and add to the brandy. Keep on until you have fruit of every season. Oranges,
pineapples and bananas can also be added the same way. Seal, and leave
until conserve thickens. (This is sumptuous served with puddings and
ice-creams.)

—Farny and Wurlitzer family
Garden Club of Cincinnati Cookbook, 1937

*Krohn Conservatory. Opened in 1933, this greenhouse in Eden Park was named for a generous
and long-term member of the Cincinnati Park Board, Irwin M. Krohn. Flowers, cultivated and
wild, are grown and cherished in Cincinnati. Citizens love visiting this conservatory in spring and
viewing the hosts of daffodils on the surrounding hillsides. Drawing by Paul Blackwell, courtesy
of Row House Gallery, Milford*

Bibliography

Anderson Township Historical Society. *Log House Cookbook*. Waverly, Iowa: G & R Publishing Co., 1980.

Beecher, Catharine Esther. *Miss Beecher's Domestic Receipt Book*. Cincinnati: Harper & Bros., 1868.

Beecher, Catharine E. and Harriet Beecher Stowe. *The Housekeeper's Manual*. Cincinnati: J. B. Ford & Co., 1874.

Bradley, Mrs. J. S. *Mrs. Bradley's Housekeeper's Guide*. Cincinnati: H. M. Rulison, 1853.

Cary, Alice and Phoebe. *The Poetical Works of Alice and Phoebe Cary, The Household Edition*. Boston: Houghton Mifflin Co., 1865.

Church of the Guardian Angels. *Angel's Food*. Cincinnati, 1974.

Christian Women's Missionary Cookbook, Liberty Chapel. Cincinnati: Press of M. Rosenthal & Co., 1921.

Clermont Country Newsletter. Loveland, 1981.

Cooperative Society of the Children's Hospital, The. *The Cincinnati Cookbook*. Cincinnati, 1966.

Day, Doris. *Her Own Story*. New York: William Morrow & Co., 1975.

Dickens on America and the Americans. Edited by Michael Slatter. Austin: University of Texas Press, 1978.

Dorcheff, George. *Tops, the Home-makers Friend Cook Book*. Norwood.

Downard, William L. *The Cincinnati Brewing Industry*. Ann Arbor: University Microfilms International, 1980.

Frank Tea and Spice Co., The. "The Wonderful World of Spices." Cincinnati.

Garden Club of Cincinnati, The. *The Garden Club of Cincinnati Cookbook*. Cincinnati: A. H. Pugh, 1937.

Glendale. *Recipes*. Cincinnati, 1935.

Gregory, James Edward. *The Chef Gregory Cookbook*. Cincinnati: F & W Publishing Co., 1972.

Howe, Ann. *The American Kitchen Directory and Housewife*. Cincinnati: Howe's Subscription Book Concern, 1868.

Hyde Park Center for Older Adults. *Bake, Simmer n' Stew*. Cincinnati, 1981.

International Folk Festival Cookbook. Cincinnati, 1979.

Mathieu, Rosella Feher. *The Herb Grower's Complete Guide.* Silverton, 1949.

McCullers, Carson. *A Member of the Wedding.* Boston: Houghton Mifflin Co., 1946.

Montgomery Assembly of God Church. *A Book of Favorite Recipes.* Cincinnati, 1981.

Neil, Edna. *Shillito's Every-day Cook-Book and Encyclopedia of Practical Recipes for Family Use.* Cincinnati, 1905.

Neil, Marion Harris. *The Story of Crisco; 250 Tested Recipes.* Cincinnati: Procter & Gamble, 1914.

New Richmond Community Club. *Rivertown Recipes.* Cincinnati, 1980.

Northside Presbyterian Church, *Choice Cookery.* Cincinnati, 1900.

Nye, Beverly K. *A Family Raised on Rainbows.* New York: Bantam, 1979.

Nye, Beverly K. *A Family Raised on Sunshine.* Cincinnati: Writer's Digest, 1977.

Ohio Library Association, Junior Member Section. *234 Extra Special Recipes.* Cincinnati, 1951.

Our Lady of Mercy Hospital Candy Stripers. *Cooking Volunteer-ily.* Cincinnati, 1967.

Our Lady of Visitation Church Sodality. *The Dinner Bell.* Cincinnati, 1976.

Joseph R. Peebles' Sons Company, The. ''Peebles Every Month.'' Cincinnati: Joseph R. Peebles' Sons, 1900-1910.

Perry, Dick. *Vas You Ever in Zinzinnati?* New York: Doubleday & Co., 1966.

Procter & Gamble. *Good Cooking Made Easy.* Des Moines: Meredith Publishing Services, 1978.

School of Housekeeping Association. *School of Housekeeping Cookbook.* Cincinnati, 1900.

Schweitzer, Father Al and Henry Gerbus. ''The History and the Story of Findlay Market and Over The Rhine.'' Cincinnati, Ohio.

Seventh Presbyterian Church. *Tested Recipes.* Cincinnati, 1916.

Seventh Presbyterian Church, Ladies of the. *Practical Receipts of Experienced Housekeepers.* Cincinnati: Robert Clarke & Co., 1878.

Sister Jean Evelyn. *A Month of Dinner Menus.* Cincinnati, 1982.

Smith & Swinney. *The House-keeper's Guide and Everybody's Handbook: Containing Over 500 New and Valuable Recipes.* Cincinnati: Stereotyped at the Franklin Type Foundry, 1864.

University of Cincinnati College of Education and Home Economics. *Rainbow of Recipes.* Cincinnati: National Alumni Association, 1978.

Unzicker, C. B. *The Household Companion and Family Receipt Book.*

Cincinnati, Unzicker Co., 1870.

Walnut Hills Christian Church, Ladies Aid Society. *Tried and...True.* Cincinnati, 1900.

White, Daniel T. *White's New Cook-Book, Embracing Temperate and Economical Receipts, for Domestic Liquors and Cookery.* Cincinnati, 1840.

Wiedemann (George) Brewing Co. *The Wiedemann Book of Unusual Recipes; Compiled from the Files of Famous Chefs.* Cincinnati: Roessler Bros., 1940.

Woman's Auxiliary of the Church of St. Michael and All Angels. *Manna a la Carta; Not All—Just Most of the Best Recipes from Homes on the Seven Hills and Gateway to the South.* Cincinnati, 1950.

Woman's City Club of Cincinnati. *Liberty Cookbook.* Cincinnati, 1917.

Woman's City Club of Cincinnati. *Recipes by Members of the Women's City Club of Cincinnati.* Cincinnati, 1952.

Wurlizter, Leonie (Farny) and Marguerite (Farny) Strobel. *A Book of Recipes Covering Three Generations of the Farny and Wurlitzer Family.* Cincinnati, 1925.

Index

221

224

Dear Friend,

If you have purchased this Cincinnati, Ohio cookbook to bring or send to another city, state or country would you be so kind as to drop me a note? As it was a once-in-a-lifetime opportunity to put it together, the pleasure continues as I learn the cities, small towns and faraway places it travels.

With great appreciation,

Mary Anna DuSablon
1366 Fay Road
Loveland, Ohio 45140